WRITER-FILES

General Editor: Simon Trussler

Associate Editor: Malcolm Page

File on
MILLER

Compiled by C. W. E. Bigsby

Methuen. London and New York

A Methuen Paperback

First published in 1987 as a paperback original
by Methuen London Ltd,
11 New Fetter Lane, London EC4P 4EE
and Methuen Inc, 29 West 35th Street,
New York, NY 10001

Typeset in 9/10 Times
by L. Anderson Typesetting
Woodchurch, Kent TN26 3TB
Printed in Great Britain
by Richard Clay (The Chaucer Press) Ltd,
Bungay, Suffolk

British Library Cataloguing in Publication Data

File on Miller — (Writer-files)
   1. Drama in English. American
   writers. Miller, Arthur, 1915-   — Critical studies
   I. Bigsby, C. W. E. (Christopher William
   Edgar) *1941-*   II. Series

   ISBN 0-413-53610-6

Contents

The theatre is, by its nature, an ephemeral art: yet it is a daunting task to track down the newspaper reviews, or contemporary statements from the writer or his director, which are often all that remain to help us recreate some sense of what a particular production was like. This series is therefore intended to make readily available a selection of the comments that the critics made about the plays of leading modern dramatists at the time of their production — and to trace, too, the course of each writer's own views about his work and his world.

In addition to combining a uniquely convenient source of such elusive *documentation*, the 'Writer-Files' series also assembles the *information* necessary for readers to pursue further their interest in a particular writer or work. Variations in quantity between one writer's output and another, differences in temperament which make some readier than others to talk about their work, and the variety of critical response, all mean that the presentation and balance of material shifts between one volume and another: but we have tried to arrive at a format for the series which will nevertheless enable users of one volume readily to find their way around any other.

Section 1, 'A Brief Chronology', provides a quick conspective overview of each playwright's life and career. *Section 2* deals with the plays themselves, arranged chronologically in the order of their composition: information on first performances, major revivals, and publication is followed by a brief synopsis (for quick reference set in slightly larger, italic type), then by a representative selection of the critical response, and of the dramatist's own comments on the play and its theme.

Section 3 offers concise guidance to each writer's work in non-dramatic forms, while *Section 4*, 'The Writer on His Work', brings together comments from the playwright himself on more general matters of construction, opinion, and artistic development. Finally, *Section 5* provides a bibliographical guide to other primary and secondary sources of further reading, among which full details will be found of works cited elsewhere under short titles, and of collected editions of the plays — but not of individual titles, particulars of which will be found with the other factual data in Section 2.

The 'Writer-Files' hope by striking this kind of balance between information and a wide range of opinion to offer 'companions' to the study of major playwrights in the modern repertoire — not in that dangerous pre-digested fashion which can too readily quench the desire to read the plays themselves, nor so prescriptively as to allow any single line of approach to predominate, but rather to encourage readers to form their own judgements of the plays in a wide-ranging context.

Arthur Miller is among the two or three dramatists of this century of a greatness that is distinctively and unmistakably American. It was perhaps no less distinctively American that he has suffered not from any lack of artistic staying-power but, quite simply, from going out of fashion. Even his early success was received, ironically, in the very terms which *Death of a Salesman*, in particular, so profoundly questioned — as a number of the reviews collected in this volume usefully remind us. He has written against the grain of prevailing assumptions, yet from a knowledge of national characteristics that made *The Crucible* no less astonishingly true to its own dramatic times than to his personal political fortunes.

He remains, formally, a highly traditional dramatist, one of the few contemporary writers willing to conceive tragedy as a viable modern genre, as also to employ the conventions of naturalism as if they were freshly-minted, at a time when many dramatists either exploited their capacity to soothe nervous susceptibilities, or rejected them in a manner also calculated to alienate precisely the audiences they should have been reaching. It is a happy accident of the planning of this series that the publication of the present volume follows so closely not only upon Miller's remarkable autobiography, *Timebends*, but also a sustained revival of interest in his plays, both new and old. It is no less happy but not in the least accidental that Miller's liberal-humanist values have survived the buffets of both political persecution and critical fashion

Whether in his most clearly-considered work or the most ephemeral off-the-cuff interview, Miller speaks with a voice that affirms our common humanity. It is ironic that so much of the interest in *Timebends* should have focused on his marriage with Marilyn Monroe: yet a century hence, if the worst features of the American sensibility have not dragged us all to extinction in the cause of freedom, the joy and giving in Monroe's best work and the concern and unsentimental compassion of Miller's will seem to characterize the very best and redeeming American qualities, so far as they can be captured by the performing arts. This volume perhaps too often demonstrates the short-sightedness of the way Miller's work has been received, but it also illuminates his ability both to compel and reward the truly attentive audience.

Simon Trussler

1915 Arthur Asher Miller born, 17 October, on East 112th Street in Harlem, New York. Parents: Augusta and Isadore.

1929 Family moves to Midwood section of Brooklyn, having felt the impact of the Depression. Father, manufacturer of women's coats and an employer of nearly a thousand workers.

1932 Graduates from Abraham Lincoln High School. Works in an automobile parts warehouse.

1934 Enrols as journalism major at the University of Michigan, Ann Arbor.

1936 *No Villain* wins $250 Avery Hopwood Award in drama from University of Michigan.

1937 *Honors at Dawn* wins $250 Avery Hopwood Award. *They Too Arise*, a revision of *No Villain*, produced at Ann Arbor. Wins Theatre Guild's Bureau of New Plays Award of $1250.

1938 *The Great Disobedience* comes second in Avery Hopwood Award. Miller graduates from university.

1939 Another revision of *They Too Arise* (now titled *The Grass Still Grows*) completed. Miller works briefly for the Federal Theatre, for which he begins a play, *The Golden Years*. Federal Theatre closed by Congress. He then writes radio plays for CBS and NBC.

1940 Marries Mary Slattery.

1941 Completes *The Golden Years* and begins a new play, *The Half-Bridge*.

1943 Completes *The Half-Bridge*.

1944 Visits army camps in search of material for *The Story of G.I. Joe*, a movie. Prose version published as *Situation Normal*. *The Man Who Had All the Luck* produced in New York. Wins Theatre Guild National Award.

1945 *Focus* published.

1947 *All My Sons* wins the New York Drama Critics Circle Award.

1949 *Death of a Salesman* wins New York Drama Critics Circle Award and Pulitzer Prize.

1950 *An Enemy of the People*, adapted from Henrik Ibsen.

1951 Writes screenplay for Columbia Pictures called *The Hook*. Asked to change crooked labour leaders into communists (the Korean War making this advisable). Refuses. Film not made.

1953 *The Crucible* wins Antoinette Perry and Donaldson Prizes.

1954 Denied passport to attend opening of *The Crucible* in Belgium.

1955 *A Memory of Two Mondays* and *A View from the Bridge* produced as double bill.

1956 Two-act version of *A View from the Bridge* produced in London. Divorced from Mary Slattery. Experience of Reno divorce the inspiration for *The Misfits*. Summoned before House Committee on Un-American Activities. Refuses to name names. Marries Marilyn Monroe.

1957 Cited for contempt of Congress: fined $500 and given a suspended 30-day sentence.

1958 Conviction for contempt of Congress quashed by Supreme Court.

1959 Gold Medal for drama from National Institute of Arts and Letters.

1960 Filming of *The Misfits*.

1961 Divorced from Marilyn Monroe. *The Misfits* released.

1962 Marries Inge Morath, a professional photographer originally from Austria.

1963 *Jane's Blanket* (a children's book) published.

1964 *After the Fall* produced in New York for the new Lincoln Centre. *Incident at Vichy* opens.

1965 Elected president of PEN International.

1968 *The Price*.

1969 Publishes *In Russia* with his wife.

1970 *Fame*.

1972 *The Creation of the World and Other Business* produced in New York.

1974 *Up from Paradise* produced at Ann Arbor.

1977 *The Archbishop's Ceiling* produced at the Kennedy Center in a revised text. *In the Country* published.

1978   Visits China. *Fame* on television.

1979   *Chinese Encounters* published.

1980   *The American Clock* opens in New York. *Playing for Time* on CBS Television.

1983   Visits Beijing in China to direct *Death of a Salesman*.

1984   *The Archbishop's Ceiling* published in original form and is produced in Cleveland. *Salesman in Beijing* published.

1985   First British production of *The Archbishop's Ceiling*, at Bristol.

1986   Visits Russia and meets Gorbachev. *The American Clock* opens at Britain's National Theatre and *The Archbishop's Ceiling* at the Royal Shakespeare Company's Pit Theatre in the Barbican Centre.

1987   *Clara* and *I Can't Remember Anything* produced at Lincoln Centre. *Timebends: a Life* published. *The Golden Years* broadcast on BBC Radio 3, a world premiere.

a: Stage Plays

No Villain/ They Too Arise/ The Grass Still Grows

Play in three acts.
First American production: 12 March 1937,
    Lydia Mendelssohn Theatre, Ann Arbor
    (dir. Frederic O. Crandall). [This play exists in at
    least four separate forms. As *No Villain* it won a Minor
    Award in Drama from the University of Michigan in 1936
    ($250).]

It tells the story of the Simon family. Abe Simon is a manufacturer of coats. His son, Ben, has joined him in the business. A second son, Arnold, is at university. A strike threatens his livelihood. As a small manufacturer he is especially vulnerable. The larger ones are prepared to hire scab labour and ally themselves with gangsters. If he is to survive he feels he has to resist the demands of his own employees and get supplies through to his customers but this creates a tension between himself and Arnold who returns from the university imbued with Marxist values. A possible solution lies in a marriage between Ben and the daughter of a large manufacturer. Abe Simon loses his business but comes to a new understanding of his society. The several versions of the play deflect the action into comedy, social play or minor tragedy.

Honors at Dawn

Play in three acts.
This play received a Minor Award for Drama from the
    University of Michigan in 1937 ($250). The judges were
    Susan Glaspell (co-founder of the Provincetown Players),

Allardyce Nicoll and Percival Wilde.
Unproduced and *unpublished*.

It is set partly at a university and partly in and around an industrial plant. The central characters are Max and Harry Zibriski, two brothers brought up on a farm but now struggling to better themselves. Harry, a spendthrift and none too serious as a student, is persuaded to spy on his fellow students by a Dean who is himself under pressure from the owner of the nearby plant who is aware of student involvement in strikes and whose own gifts to the university give him the power to influence events. Brother is set against brother. The play ends with Max wounded and probably dying, shot for defending the rights of his worker friends.

The Great Disobedience

Play in three acts.
First American production: University of Michigan laboratory
   production, 1938.
Unpublished.

Set in Mount Warren prison 'somewhere in the center of the United States', this play concerns the efforts of a psychiatrist, Dr. Karl Mannheim, to reform a brutal and brutalizing system. When a doctor friend and classmate is sentenced for performing an abortion on a young woman worker — herself the victim of a ruthless industrial combine — the psychiatrist is urged to help him by the man's wife. But Mannheim's efforts, despite an apparent victory, prove worthless as he comes to realize that the influence of that same company extends to the judicial and penal system itself.

The Golden Years

Play in three acts.

Produced: BBC Radio 3, 1987.

Written in 1939, this is a study of the conflict between Montezuma and Cortez. Both men are in thrall to a myth; both have dealt in violence. Montezuma, however, having conquered the known world, now looks for something more, a trans- substantiation, a dialogue with the gods. He sees Cortez as a returned deity, brushing aside resistance imperiously. Cortez is in search of gold and power. In a sense he, too, aspires to godhead. Both are locked into a ruinous logic. A displaced account of events in Europe, where Miller saw governments apparently transfixed and frozen into inaction in the face of Hitler's absolutism, the play is also a poetic debate over the fallibility of the human race whose evil cannot be expunged by its equal desire for transcendence.

The play was interesting on several levels: Americans quite rightly feel retrospectively guilt-stricken about the European impact on the New World, but in 1940 Miller was more propagandist in his aims, painting Cortez as a Hitler-figure who would devastate an innocent New World, though innocent is perhaps not quite the word for an Aztec empire which was violent, brutal and rotten with superstition.

Alan Ryan, *Sunday Telegraph*, 8 November 1987

The Golden Years is a baroque piece, with proper attention given to excitement and tension, in the case, for instance, of the helmets of Cortez and Quetzalcoatl — if they were alike, the invaders were indeed gods. There are even two quasi-romances. Cortez's historic one between Montezuma's daughter, Tecuichpo and Cortez's captain, Alvarado. Like Atahuallpa, Montezuma found himself fighting his own brother.

The alleged object of the operation was the conversion of the Aztecs; 'I could have been a Christian', Montezuma says, dying from his own people's arrows after pleading for the escape of the invaders, 'but now I see the Christians are debased people' — and as the Christians are concerned above all with stealing the Aztec wealth, there was something in that judgment.

B. A. Young, *Financial Times*, 7 November 1987

It is not curiosity value alone — though it has plenty of that, because this is the first time Arthur Miller's 47-year-old play has ever been performed — that gives tonight's broadcast of *The Golden Years* its particular excitement. What really matters is that this early Miller has flashes of psychological insight (and certainly of poetry) that are worthy to stand alongside anything in later Miller. His chronicle about the confrontation between the Aztec emperor Montezuma and the Spanish *conquistador* Cortez inevitably calls to mind Peter Shaffer's *The Royal Hunt of the Sun* (Inca king Atahuallpa confronting Spanish *conquistador* Pizarro). Put the two plays side by side, try to forget the breath-taking staging of Shaffer's play, and Miller has the edge on the competition. Though characteristic of the playwright, it is of secondary importance that Miller sees Cortez as a sixteenth century Hitler. The clash between the bloody invader (John Shrapnel) and the noble savage (Ronald Pickup) is staged outside historical time because it springs from the recurring theme of one ideological attitude being subverted by another.

Peter Davalle, *The Times*, 6 November 1987

Already in 1939, before the war began and fresh out of college, I had written a large tragedy about Montezuma's destruction at the hands of Cortez. Montezuma convinced himself that the strange white creatures who had come out of the ocean were fated to be his masters and at the same time to apotheosize him to godhood now that he had, as he believed, led his Aztecs to the conquest of all the known world and had nothing left to do with his life. Very differently put, the same question is raised in both plays *The Golden Years* and *The Man Who Had All the Luck* — the dreamlike irreality of success and power. Both plays, it should be said, were at the same time referring to the paralysis of will in the democracies as Hitler moved week by week to the domination of all Europe.

Arthur Miller, *Timebends*

Listen My Children

Written (1939) with Norman Rosten, fellow graduate from the
University of Michigan. A 'comedy satire with music'.
Unproduced and *unpublished.*

The Half-Bridge

Play in three acts.
Unproduced and *unpublished*.

Written between 1941 and 1943, the play is set on and around a merchant vessel berthed in the harbour at New Orleans. The Captain and his crew seem to be working for a German spy ring. The German spymaster proposes that the ship should operate as a raider, but his real plan involves insurance fraud. The central character is Mark Donegal, self-destructive, in search of danger as a route to meaning. He falls in love with Anna Walden who is herself in flight from the law. Eventually the forces of life prevail and they escape the commercial venality and political terrors which had menaced them.

That They May Win

Play in one act.
First American production: amateur production in New York in 1943-4 season.
Published: in *The Best One-Act Plays of 1944*, ed. Margaret Mayorga (New York, 1945).

A play about war veterans which insists that politics is a natural extension of private rights and responsibilities.

The Man Who Had All the Luck

Play in three acts with four scenes.
First American production: Forrest Th., New York, 23 Nov. 1944 (staged by Joseph Fields; with Karl Swenson as David Beeves).
First London production: Tower Th., Canonbury, London, 28 April 1960 (dir. Charles Marowitz).
Published: in *Cross Section*, ed. Edwin Seaver (New York, 1944).

The play turns on the conceit that David Beeves is a man for whom everything turns out well, albeit partly because of an act of minor dishonesty. The irony is that the more things go in his direction the more vulnerable he feels, until he eventually decides to precipitate a disaster, almost as though it is necessary to get it out of the way. In the original version everything ends happily. In 1986, however, Miller revised the ending, and in this version David Beeves commits suicide.

The Man Who Had All the Luck is about a fellow who tries a lot of things and they all click, but he keeps thinking that sooner or later something will flop because it stands to reason he's got to pay up in the end. Arthur Miller, the newcomer who wrote the play, has done all his paying-up right off the bat. His first offering tries a lot of things — too many by far — and most of them flop.

And now I hope Mr. Miller will go right back to work writing another piece, for he has a sense of theatre and a real if undeveloped way of making stage characters talk and act human.

Almost all these elements have something of interest in them — but they won't stick together and make a whole play. Mr. Miller would have been much happier today had he taken just one part of his plot — the part about the ballplayer — and made three acts of it.

John Chapman, *New York Daily News*, 24 Nov. 1944

There can be no doubt that as an evening in the theatre *The Man Who Had All the Luck* contains a certain amount of merit. There are some good performances and careful staging and one or two effective moments. The fact that they have not been multiplied is the new play's misfortune, for the author and director — Arthur Miller and Joseph Fields — at least have been trying to do something away from the theatre's usual stencils. But in the Forrest's current tenant they have not edited out the confusion of the script nor its somewhat jumbled philosophies, nor have they kept it from running over into the ridiculous now and then. *The Man Who Had All the Luck* can be set down as a play which tried, but which did not come off — through luck or whatever.

Lewis Nichols, *New York Times*, 24 Nov. 1944

This play was an investigation to discover what exact part a man played in his own fate. It deals with a young man in a small town who, by the time he is in his mid-twenties, owns several growing businesses, has married the girl he loves, is the father of a child he has always wanted, and is daily becoming convinced that as his desires are gratified he is causing to accumulate around his own head an invisible but nearly palpable fund, so to speak, of retribution. The law of life, as he observes life around him, is that people are always frustrated in some important regard; and he conceives that he must be too, and the play is built around his conviction of impending disaster. The disaster never comes, even when, in effect, he tries to bring it on in order to survive it and find peace. Instead, he comes to believe in his own superiority, and in his remarkable ability to succeed.

Now, more than a decade later, it is possible for me to see that far from being a waste and a failure this play was a preparation, and possibly a necessary one, for those that followed, especially *All My Sons* and *Death of a Salesman*, and this for many reasons.

What I saw, without laboring the details, was that two of the characters, who had been friends in the previous drafts, were logically brothers and had the same father. Had I known then what I know now I could have saved myself a lot of trouble. The play was impossible to fix because the overt story was only tangential to the secret drama its author was quite unconsciously trying to write. But in writing of the father-son relationship and of the son's search for his relatedness there was a fullness of feeling I had never known before; a a crescendo was struck with a force I could almost touch. The crux of *All My Sons*, which would not be written until nearly three years later, was formed; and the roots of *Death of a Salesman* were sprouted.

The form of *All My Sons* is a reflection and an expression of several forces, of only some of which I was conscious. I desired above all to write rationally, to write so that I could tell the story of the play to even an unlettered person and spark a look of recognition on his face. The accusation I harbored against the earlier play was that it could not make sense to common-sense people.

Arthur Miller, Introduction to *Collected Plays*

All My Sons

Play in three acts.

First American production: Coronet Th., 29 Jan. 1947 (presented by Elia Kazan, Harold Clurman, and Walter Fried; with Ed Begley as Joe Keller, Beth Merrill as Kate, Arhur Kennedy as Chris, and Lois Wheeler as Ann.

First London production: Lyric Th., Hammersmith, 11 May 1948 (with Joseph Calleia as Joe, Margalo Gillmore as Kate,

Richard Leech as Chris and Harriette Johns as Ann).
*Published:*Reynal and Hitchcock, New York, 1947. Also in
Arthur Miller's Collected Plays, Vol. I., New York: Viking 1957.
Collected Plays, London, 1958. Harmondsworth: Penguin, 1961.
Film version: Universal International, 1948.

Joe Keller is a manufacturer of aircraft engines. In the course of production a fault occurs but, committed to profit, he allows the defective parts to be fitted to airforce planes where they result in fatal crashes. Rather than go to jail himself he allows his business partner to take the blame. One of his sons, himself an airforce pilot, dies in the war, though his wife can never accept his death and for that reason equally cannot accept that her dead son's fiancee should have transferred her affections to the other son, Chris. He, in turn, has to convince her that his brother will not be coming back so that he is free to marry Ann. Then the couple discover evidence of Joe Keller's culpability and confront him with it and with evidence that his airforce son had committed suicide out of shame. The result is that Joe Keller himself commits suicide. It is a play equally about the corrupting power of greed and the destructiveness of an idealism untinged with humanity.

'With the production of *All My Sons* at the Coronet last evening, the theatre has acquired a genuine new talent. Arthur Miller, who wrote *The Man Who Had All the Luck* in 1944, brings something fresh and exciting into the drama. He has written an honest, forceful drama about a group of people caught up in a monstrous swindle that has caused the death of twenty-one Army pilots because of defectively manufactured cylinder heads.

Told against the single setting of an ordinary American backyard, it is a pitiless analysis of character that gathers momentum all evening and concludes with both logic and dramatic impact.

Mr. Miller's talent is many sided. Writing pithy yet unselfconscious dialogue, he has created his characters vividly, plucking them out of the run of American society, but presenting them as individuals with hearts and minds of their own. He is also a skilful technician. His drama is a piece of expert dramatic construction. Mr. Miller has woven his characters into a tangle of plot that springs naturally out of the circumstances of life today. Having set the stage he drives the play along by natural crescendo to a startling and terrifying climax.

Fortunately, *All My Sons* is produced and directed by people who value it and who have given it a taut and pulsing performance with actors of sharp and knowing intelligence. It is always gratifying to see old hands succeed in the theatre. But there is something uncommonly exhilarating in the spectacle of a new writer bringing unusual gifts to the theatre under the sponsorship of a director with taste and enthusiasm. In the present instance, the director is Elia Kazan.

Brooks Atkinson, *New York Times*, 30 Jan. 1947

All My Sons is a play of high voltage, charged with things to say. No civilian, past or present, will find himself immune from its comment. The play in its broadest sense demands a realization of the big inter-dependence of people. Specifically it tells of the hideous lesson learned by a man who thought he could gamble with strange lives and benefit his own family. The play unfolds with unusual tenseness. The conflicts are vital, never simply black and white. The people are torn by the webs of their relationship and can seldom take a clean-cut stand against each other.

Arthur Miller has written this forceful play in simple, clean, human speech. Poorly paraphrased, Chris's realization from the war is that unless you are conscious every time you ride in a car or eat a bite of food that you owe a debt of gratitude to the dead, it is loot with blood on it.

All My Sons is a play where the family, and the neighbors and the term 'next door', are vital elements in everybody's picture. These are usual people with usual ambitions.

The strength of the play is the revelation that a wide horizon is becoming a necessity for intimate happiness.

William Hawkins, *New York World Telegram*, 30 Jan. 1947

Of *All My Sons* it can be said immediately that it is a drama of force and passion. These are no small attributes in the modern theatre, which is sometimes afraid of its own emotional strength. Furthermore, it has the courage of its climaxes, being perfectly willing to go in for honest theatrical emphasis whenever it feels called upon to do so. On all of these scores it and its playwright, Arthur Miller, deserve high commendation. That it is likewise an extremely uneven play is hardly to be disputed. While some of it is powerful and inescapably impressive, other sections are clumsy and sometimes a trifle embarrassing, an understandable weakness in dramatic works which shoot fairly high. Indeed *All My Sons* is overwrought, hysterical, over-plotted and unwieldy, as well as impassioned and impressive. It is not, I fear, a very good play or an entirely convincing one since its cargo of plot, characterization, symbolism and social crusading is too large and is piled up too clumsily for such a comparatively ramshackle dramatic vessel. Yet, for all its undoubted weaknesses it is a drama which is always to be respected and which often achieves scenes of a remarkable degree of theatrical excitement.

Richard Watts Jr., *New York Post*, 30 Jan. 1947

Out of this urgent, this immediate material, Arthur Miller has fashioned an engrossing play which after a fumbling beginning, rises relentlessly to its denouement. There is, if Messrs Clurman and Kazan will excuse me, an Ibsenesque quality to the craftsmanship of the rising young playwright's narrative. In *All My Sons* he creates his characters while they in turn, create the post-World War II problems which stem honestly out of them. . . .

Robert Garland, *Journal American*, 30 Jan. 1947

All My Sons, put on last night at the Coronet, is a play to be welcomed and respected, one that has a great deal to say on the subject of responsibility in wartime, and one that says it vigorously. The author, the oncoming Arthur Miller, is a young dramatist who can put explosive force into his scenes.

This new drama begins somewhat exasperatingly. It is occasionally a fitful and spasmodic play, cluttered with many story threads and veering now and then from one sub-plot to another, but when it is concentrating on its main issue, which is the guilt of a wartime airplane parts manufacturer, the father of two sons, it has extraordinary poignancy and power. . . .

All My Sons, brought forth by the new producing combination of Harold Clurman, Elia Kazan and Walter Fried, in association with Herbert H. Harris, is an intelligent and thoughtful drama. The over-all effect is one of force, an almost unendurable force, in many scenes. And in Miller the Broadway theatre has a new playwright of enormous promise.

Ward Morehouse, *The Sun*, 30 Jan. 1947

With his second Broadway play, Arthur Miller seems to me to stand easily first among our new generation of playwrights. . . . The really disappointing thing about most of our 'promising' playwrights is the awful mediocrity of their minds, the too great simplicity of their aims. Mr. Miller is more interesting than they, so that even his faults seem more interesting. If *All My Sons* creates an effect of congestion, it is because it has some notion of complexity. If matters sometimes get overheated, it is because they are not born of cold calculation. Even what is unconvincing about his people is partly due to their not being cut from whole cloth. But, faults or not, *All My Sons* is on the whole a compelling play. Mr. Miller has brought to it three things very vital to a serious stage work; he has a dramatic sense, he has a human sense, and he has a moral sense. And these things converge upon a situation in itself provocative. . . .

He is not just another playwright angrily shaking his fist at greed and unscrupulousness. Indeed, his tone, though passionate, is not at all polemical. He is dealing with the complex problem of human responsibility, and dealing with it in very human terms. He gets at men's morality through their psychology. Joe Keller has rationalized his misdeeds by a callous acceptance of the American gospel of practicality: and he has discounted any responsibility toward society by stressing his responsibility to his family, to seeing that it gets ahead in the world. And others, too, in the play are beset by guilts and divided loyalties with the moral compromises that result from them. Far from creating any villains, Mr. Miller shows how close 'villains' are to normally self-interested people. Not cruelty and hate, but self-interest and even self-preservation, prove the greatest menaces to society — if only because they forge the most plausible sanctions for acting irresponsibly. More than at first it seems to, *All My Sons* slashes at all the defective parts of our social morality: but most of all it slashes at the unsocial nature of family loyalties, of protecting or aggrandizing the tribe at the expense of society at large.

Louis Kronenberger, *PM Reviews*, 31 Jan 1947

All My Sons has often been called a moral play, and it is that, but the concept of morality is not quite as purely ethical as it has been made to appear, nor is it so in the plays that follow. That the deed of Joe Keller at issue in *All My Sons* is his having been the cause of the death of pilots in war obscures the other kind of morality in which the play is primarily interested. Morality is probably a faulty word to use in the connection, but what I was after was the wonder in the fact that consequences of actions are as real as the actions themselves, yet we rarely take them into consideration as we perform actions, and we cannot hope to do so fully when we must always act with only partial knowledge of consequences. Joe Keller's trouble, in a word, is not that he cannot tell right from wrong but that his cast of mind cannot admit that he, personally, has any viable connection with his world, his universe, or his society. He is not a partner in society, but an incorporated member, so to speak, and you cannot sue personally the officers of a corporation. I hasten to make clear here that I am not merely speaking of a literal corporation but the concept of a man's becoming a function of production or distribution to the point where his personality becomes divorced from the actions it propels.

The fortress which *All My Sons* lays siege to is the fortress of unrelatedness. It is an assertion not so much of a morality in terms of right and wrong, but of a moral world's being such because men cannot walk away from certain of their deeds.

Arthur Miller, Introduction to *Collected Plays*

Death of a Salesman

Play in two acts.

First American production: Morosco Th., New York, 10 Feb. 1949 (dir. Elia Kazan; with Lee J. Cobb as Willy, Mildred Dunnock as Linda, Arthur Kennedy as Biff, and Cameron Mitchell as Happy).

First London production: Phoenix Th., London, 28 July 1949 (with Paul Muni as Willy, Katharine Alexander as Linda, Kevin McCarthy as Biff, and Frank Maxwell as Happy).

Revival: Lyttelton Th., London, 20 Sept. 1979 (dir. Michael Rudman; with Warren Mitchell as Willy). New York, 1984 (dir. Michael Rudman; with Dustin Hoffman as Willy).

Published: New York: Viking, 1949. Harmondsworth: Penguin, 1961.

Film version: Columbia Pictures, 1952.

Record: Caedmon, 1965.

Willy Loman is an ageing salesman whose grasp on the reality of his life is slipping away from him. Having raised two sons — Biff and Happy — to share his faith in the American Dream he feels guilty because his own infidelity had so disillusioned Biff that he had turned his back on the pursuit of success. To preserve a sense of himself, independent of his father's dreams, it is necessary for Biff to cut himself free from Willy; to assuage his sense of guilt it is necessary for Willy to embrace his son and convince him of the reality of the fantasies which he has himself spent a lifetime pursuing. At the end of the play Willy commits suicide in the conviction that he is leaving behind the proceeds of an insurance policy which will provide the basis for the

21

success which had evaded him and which seems to be evading them. His wife, Linda, is baffled by the gesture which is nonetheless a logical extension of a life-long sacrifice of selfhood to a dream which had been the central action of, and justification for, his existence.

A great play of our day has opened at the Morosco. *Death of a Salesman*, by Arthur Miller, has majesty, sweep and shattering dramatic impact. As it has been staged by Elia Kazan and consummately performed by Lee J. Cobb, Arthur Kennedy, Mildred Dunnock and all their associates, it is a soaring tragedy. There is always pertinence to this tale of a defeated old drummer coming to the dead end of his career. A terrible documentation has been leavened with bursts of wild humor and more than one moment of touching grandeur, while the fluent scenes build inexorably to the climax. With Jo Mielziner's inspired setting and lighting, the offering is theatre of the first order. . . .

Miller is no novice at dramaturgy, his *All My Sons* having won a Critics Circle Award, but he has grown enormously in artistic stature since that earlier play. There is lucidity, eloquence and deep feeling in *Death of a Salesman* which makes it far more than a good job of craftsmanship. The story of Willy Loman, who lived for a strange dream and tried to have it realized by a worthless son, while destroying the boy, has its roots deep in the complex structure of contemporary existence. The author has attacked his theme relentlessly. But he has had the gift to give his work exaltation as well as tragic meaning. The gradual disintegration of the salesman is the core of the drama, yet it has a multitude of facets.

Howard Barnes, New York Herald Tribune, 11 Feb. 1949

Arthur Miller has written a superb drama. From every point of view *Death of a Salesman*, which was acted at the Morosco last evening, is rich and memorable drama. It is so simple in style and so inevitable in theme that it scarcely seems like a thing that has been written and acted. For Mr. Miller has looked with compassion into the hearts of some ordinary Americans and quietly transferred their hope and anguish to the theatre. . . .

Two seasons ago Mr. Miller's *All My Sons* looked like the work of an honest and able playwright. In comparison with the new drama, that seems like a contrived play now. For *Death of a Salesman* has the flow and spontaneity of a suburban epic that may not be intended as poetry but becomes poetry in spite of itself because Mr. Miller has drawn it out of so many intangible sources. . . .

Writing like a man who understands people, Mr. Miller has no moral precepts to offer and no solutions of the salesman's problems. He is full of pity, but he brings no piety to it. Chronicler of one frowzy corner of the American scene, he evokes a wraithlike tragedy out of it that spins through the many scenes of his play and gradually envelops the audience. . . .

Brooks Atkinson, *New York Times*, 11 Feb. 1949

Death of a Salesman which was presented last evening at the Morosco is a very fine work in the American theatre. I cannot urge it upon you too strongly. To see it is to have one of those unforgettable times in which all is right and nothing is wrong. . . .

The author is Arthur Miller, who showed promise when he wrote *The Man Who Had All the Luck* and who showed more promise with *All My Sons*. In last evening's drama he has shown something new and more profound — a pre-occupation with people rather than with ideas. He has discovered that we go to the theatre to see people, and that if he can make us love them or weep for them he has given us all we ask. . . .

Mr. Miller has been praised before for the 'naturalness' of his dialogue. His writing in *Death of a Salesman* is splendid — terse, always in character and always aimed toward the furtherance of his drama.

John Chapman, *Daily News*, 11 Feb. 1949

Here's my true report that yesterday at the Morosco the first-night congregation made no effort to leave the theatre at the final curtain fall of Arthur Miller's *Death of a Salesman*. It's meant to make known to you the prevailing emotional impact of the new play by the author of *All My Sons*.

As a theatre reporter I'm telling you how that first-night congregation remained in its seats beyond the final curtain fall. For a period somewhat shorter than it seemed an expectant silence hung over the crowded auditorium. Then believe me tumultuous appreciation shattered the hushed expectancy.

It was and will remain one of the lasting rewards that I as a professional theatregoer have received in a long full life of professional theatregoing. In *Death of a Salesman*, Arthur Miller had given that first night congregation no ordinary new play to praise, to damn, or to ignore.

This, his most iconoclastic composition, is not easy on its congregation, first-night or later on. In writing what he wants to write he has asked — demanded, rather — your sympathy as a fellow member of the bedevilled human race and your attention as an intelligent collaborator

23

as well. These, with everything else that's good, the author of *Death of a Salesman* received whole-heartedly last night. The play's playwright and playgoers were worthy of each other.

Robert Garland, *Journal American*, 11 Feb. 1949

Arthur Miller, who was revealed as a 'promising' playwright in his successful *All My Sons* a couple of seasons ago, reaches fulfilment as a dramatist of individuality and power in *Death of a Salesman*, which had its eagerly awaited opening at the Morosco last night. Gone is Mr. Miller's rather laboured obeisance to Ibsen, and in its place is a definite quality of his own, a kind of cold intellectual clarity mixed with simple and unashamed emotional force. Under Elia Kazan's vigorous and perceptive direction *Death of a Salesman* emerges as easily the best and most important new American play of the year.

Its title has the virtue not only of being striking and provocative, but of telling forthrightly what the drama is about. Mr. Miller is describing the last days of a man who is forced to face the terrible fact that he is a failure, that his vague success ideal has crumbled and that his sons on whose respect and admiration he has counted have only contempt for him. With the utter collapse of his world there is nothing for him to do but die. The story is as simple as that and there is such truth in it that it is hard to see how any sensitive playgoer of mature years can fail to find something of himself in the mirror it holds up to life.

Only the most fatuous observer could think of *Death of a Salesman* as a propaganda play and yet it manages to go deeply enough into contemporary values to be valid and frightening social criticism. Mr. Miller looks upon the salesman ideal of success with an angry but discerning eye, and he sees its hollowness and its treachery. Poor Willy Loman, who thought that for a successful salesman popularity and good fellowship were all, and tried to teach his sons what he believed was his wisdom, is a completely credible victim of a prevailing code, as the encroachment of old age destroys its shabby plausibility.

To the telling of his painful story, the playwright brings a direct, unadorned and starkly effective prose style that has nothing fancy, mystic or studiously poetic about it. Yet with all its realisms, *Death of a Salesman* is by no means simply a realistic play. While its action covers the last two days of the protagonist's life it ranges back and forth through his past, and it does so with a stream-of-consciousness technique which might have been ornate but is managed with no suggestion of pretentiousness. Set down with frank emotion, the new play is, I suspect, something to make strong men weep and think.

Richard Watts Jr., *New York Post*, 11 Feb. 1949

Death of a Salesman is a play written along the lines of the finest classical tragedy. It is the revelation of a man's downfall, a destruction whose roots are entirely in his own soul. The play builds to an immutable conflict where there is no resolution for this man in this life.

The play is a fervent query into the great American competitive dream of success, as it strips to the core a castaway from the race for recognition and money.

The failure of a great potential could never be so moving or so universally understandable as is the fate of Willy Loman, because his complete happiness could have been so easy to attain. He is an artisan who glories in a manual effort and can be proud of the sturdy fine things he puts together out of wood and cement.

Often plays have been written that crossed beyond physical actuality into the realm of memory and imagination, but it is doubtful if any has so skillfully transcended the limits of real time and space. One cannot term the chronology here a flashback technique, because the transitions are so immediate and logical.

Sometimes Willy recalls the chance he once had to join his rich adventurous brother, and as his desperation increases he begs Ben for some explanation of his deep confusion.

These illuminations of the man are so exquisitely moulded into the form of the play that it sweeps along like a powerful tragic symphony. The actors are attuned to the text as if they were distinct instruments. Themes rise and fade, are varied and repeated. Again as in music, an idea may be introduced as a faint echo and afterwards developed to its fullest part in the big scheme.

William Hawkins, *New York World Telegram*, 11 February 1949

An explosion of emotional dynamite was set off last evening in the Morosco by producers Kermit Bloomgarden and Walter Fried. In fashioning *Death of a Salesman* for them, author Arthur Miller and director Elia Kazan have collaborated on as exciting and devastating a theatrical blast as the nerves of modern playgoers can stand.

The new arrival is composed of essentially the same materials used by the Greek tragedians of the Golden Age. It gains power as it progresses. It moves relentlessly to its inevitable conclusion. It stirred the first night audience so deeply that sobs were heard throughout the auditorium, and handkerchiefs were kept busy wiping away tears. . . .

Take our advice, and rush to the Morosco early this morning to purchase tickets for *Death of a Salesman*. Should you delay, you're going to have to wait to obtain them. For, in our opinion, Miller has written not only a distinguished play but a terrific hit.

Robert Coleman, *Daily Mirror*, 11 Feb. 1949

Arthur Miller's *Death of a Salesman*, exhibited last evening at the Morosco, is the most powerful and most exciting play that the season has revealed to date. A merciless and withering drama, it is packed with intensity and genuine theater. Elia Kazan has staged it magnificently.

Playwright Miller, whose stature as a dramatist is now immeasurably increased, presents a searching examination of the life of a little man and of his relationship with his family. He does so with vivid and beautiful writing in a series of scenes, some of which are numbing in sheer power.

This new play by the author of *All My Sons* has pathos, pitilessness, violence, tenderness, humour and vehemence.

Arthur Miller has written a poignant, shattering and devastating drama in *Death of a Salesman*. When the living theatre soars it dwarfs all competitive mediums. It soared last night at the Morosco. Miller's new play is a triumph in writing, in acting and in stagecraft.

Ward Morehouse, *The Sun*,
11 Feb. 1949

A serious theme is entertaining to the extent that it is not trifled with, not cleverly angled, but met in head-on collision. [The audience] will not consent to suffer while the creators stand by with tongue in cheek. They have a way of knowing. Nobody can blame them.

And there have been certain disappointments, one above all. I am sorry the self-realization of the older son, Biff, is not a weightier counterbalance to Willy's disaster in the audience's mind.

And certain things are more clearly known, or so it seems now. We want to give of ourselves, and yet all we train for is to take, as though nothing less will keep the world at a safe distance. Every day we contradict our will to create, which is to give. The end of man is not security, but without security we are without the elementary condition of humaneness.

To me the tragedy of Willy Loman is that he gave his life, or sold it, in order to justify the waste of it. It is the tragedy of a man who did believe that he alone was not meeting the qualifications laid down for mankind by those clean-shaven frontiersmen who inhabit the peaks of broadcasting and advertising offices. From those forests of canned goods high up near the sky, he heard the thundering command to succeed as it ricocheted down the newspaper-lined canyons of his city, heard not a human voice, but a wind of a voice to which no human can reply in kind, except to stare into the mirror at a failure.

Arthur Miller, *New York Times*,
5 Feb. 1950

An Enemy of the People

Play in three acts.
First American production: Broadhurst Th., New York, 28 Dec. 1950
    (dir. Robert Lewis; with Morris Carnovsky as Peter Stockmann).
Published: New York: Viking, 1951. In *Four Plays of Our Time*,
    London: Macmillan, 1960.
Record: Caedmon, 1970.

An adaptation of Ibsen's play in which Peter Stockmann finds himself at odds with his community as he reveals the pollution of the town's water supply, an act which places moral duty at odds with what is thought of narrowly as civic responsibility since this is a spa town dependent on those who are attracted by its reputation for health-giving waters.

Papa Ibsen has had a shot in the arm. Taking a literal translation of *An Enemy of the People* as the source material, Arthur Miller has made a new adaptation, which was put on at the Broadhurst Theatre last evening. Next to *King Lear*, it is the bitterest play in town, and it is also a vast improvement over the lugubrious Archer translation that for years has represented Ibsen to us in English.

Without a knowledge of the original Norwegian, no one can tell how much of the surface of the drama is Ibsen or Miller. But the theme of the honest man standing for his convictions against the mob is pure Ibsen, angry and defiant. It is Ibsen speaking a good word for the truth of the individual and shaking his fist at society. Since it falls into none of the current political categories, it is a stirring thing to hear in the theatre and a good deal fresher than most of the political thought of today.

By dispensing with the previous English translation, Mr. Miller has released the anger and scorn of the father of realism. But don't overlook the passion that the current performance contributes. For Robert Lewis has directed it with the fury of moral melodrama, and Frederic March plays it with a breadth and volume that are overwhelming. You may find the impact too stunning, since it calls attention to itself. Sometimes it makes you uncomfortably aware of the mechanics of the acting and the arbitrariness of the playwriting. But no doubt that is a matter of personal taste. For you can hardly escape the power and excitement of a bold drama audaciously let loose in the theatre by actors and stage people who are not afraid of their strength.

Brooks Atkinson, *New York Times*, 29 Dec. 1950

And I believe this play could be alive for us because its central theme is, in my opinion, the central theme of our social life today. Simply, it is the question of whether the democratic guarantees protecting political minorities ought to be set aside in time of crisis. More personally, it is the question of whether one's vision of the truth ought to be a source of guilt at a time when the mass of men condemn it as a dangerous and devilish lie. It is an enduring theme — in fact, possibly the most enduring of all Ibsen's themes — because there never was, nor will there ever be, an organized society able to countenance calmly the individual who insists that he is right while the vast majority is absolutely wrong.

Throughout the play I have tried to peel away its trappings of the moment, its relatively accidental details which ring the dull green tones of Victorianism, and to show that beneath them there still lives the terrible wrath of Henrik Ibsen, who could make a play as men make watches, precisely, intelligently, and telling not merely the minute and the hour but the age.

Arthur Miller, *An Enemy of the People*
(New York: Viking, 1951), p. 7-12

The more familiar I became with the play, the less comfortable I felt with one or two of its implications. Though Dr. Stockmann fights admirably for absolute licence to tell society the truth, he goes on to imply the existence of an unspecified elite that can prescribe what people are to believe. For a democrat this was rather a large pill, until I recalled myself telling the meeting of Marxists years earlier that an artist had the duty to claim new territory, and that if I had obeyed either the Party line or the shibboleths of the national press during the war, I could not have written *All My Sons* — which, now that the war was over, was being praised for its courage, its insights, and its truth. Ibsen-Stockmann was simply making the artist's immemorial claim to point man into the unknown.

Still, it is indefensible in a democratic society, albeit the normal practice to ascribe superior prescience to a self-elected group, and the tangle only gets worse when Ibsen draws a parallel with biological selection, even introducing an element of breeding into the matter. Indeed, the great man himself had found it necessary to back away from the play's implied social Darwinism by going before a trade union meeting in Norway and assuring the resentful members that he was only calling for recognition of a spiritual avant-garde with no power over other people but merely the right to advance new ideas and discoveries without a majority vote. In the play, however, this demurrer remained somewhat less forthright, it seemed to me.

And so I cut across the problem to its application to our moment in America — the need, if not the holy right, to resist the pressure to conform. It was a full-blown production with solid sets of a Freddie March in the flood of his considerable art, and bristling with his private anger besides. Eldridge did her damndest to rub some colour into the rather grey role of Stockmann's worried, faithful wife. If Lewis erred, it was in encouraging a certain self-indulgent picturesqueness and a choreographed quality, especially in the stirring crowd scenes where March stood over the townspeople with arms spread out like Christ on the cross, something dangerously off-putting in what was a teaching play to start with, but these were quibbles of my own. The production was strong and forthright, and in dozens of other productions in coming years the same script would electrify audiences, though on Broadway it never caught fire.

Arthur Miller, *Timebends*

The Crucible

Play in four acts.
First American production: Martin Beck Th., New York, 22 Jan. 1953
   (staged by Jed Harris; with Arthur Kennedy as John Proctor,
   Beatrice Straight as Elizabeth Proctor and Madeleine Sherwood as
   Abigail Williams).
First British production: Theatre Royal, Bristol, 9 Nov. 1954
   (dir. Warren Jenkins; with Edgar Wreford as John Proctor,
   Rosemary Harris as Elizabeth Proctor and Pat Sandys as
   Abigail Williams).
Published: New York: Viking, 1953. London: Cresset, 1956.
Film version: Films de France, 1957 (*Les Sorcieres de Salem*,
   script by Jean-Paul Sartre).
Revival: Old Vic, London, Jan. 1965 (dir. Laurence Olivier).
   Comedy Th., London, Mar. 1981 (dir. Bill Bryden).

Produced during the McCarthy witch hunt of the early fifties, this was seen as a political parable, but in fact Miller had been attracted by the story many years before. John Proctor's affair with the young Abigail Williams is a thing of the past when the play begins; but not for Abigail. So that when witchcraft is suggested, as one of a group of girls found playing at black magic in the woods goes into a catatonic trance, she seizes the opportunity to get her revenge on John's wife, Elizabeth.

29

Indeed, in the seventeenth century New England community of Salem witchcraft constitutes both a credible charge and an opportunity to pay off old scores. Soon, many of the worthier citizens are on their way to the gallows. John Proctor tries to save his wife by confessing to adultery and hence underscoring Abigail's motive in bringing the accusation. But, seeking to protect him, she denies this, and thus condemns them both to death. Proctor is offered the opportunity to confess and thus save his life. He is tempted to do so but in the end loses his life to preserve his name and, incidentally, his soul.

Arthur Miller's *The Crucible*, which opened at the Martin Beck last night, is a drama of emotional power and impact. In it, the author of *Death of a Salesman* is contemplating the rise of mass hysteria and intolerance as represented by the horrible Salem witch trials of 1692, and, although he clearly would not be averse to having his spectators notice certain disquieting resemblances to present-day conditions, he doesn't press the parallels too closely. The result is a hardhitting and effective play that demands and deserves audience attention, even though it lacks some of the compelling excellence I had expected of it.

This is certainly not to say that *The Crucible* is without the spirit and eloquence that we have come to expect of Mr. Miller. Almost throughout, the play's emotional forthrightness grips the attention and holds it amid a succession of scenes of unrelenting excitement. It is written with feeling and indignation, and the importance of what it is saying by implication gives it dignity, largeness and inescapable distinction. . . .

The Crucible, Arthur Miller's agitating new melodrama, refers to the purification of men's conscience through terrible trial.

Mr. Miller goes back to the seventeenth-century witchcraft trials in Salem, and tells a convulsive dramatic story. How close to real sources the play remains, is unimportant. It is big and bold and very theatrical. Sometimes it is very neat. The chief instigator of the fatal business is motivated by lust for her former employer, hoping to destroy his wife and replace her.

Sometimes the scales are over-balanced as when the court is painted so bloodthirsty that the malicious accusers pale by comparison to it.

But then the drama spirals in, from the story of a community whose repressions invite mass insanity, to the finer struggle of one man with his conscience. Condemned along with many others, the young farmer whose lust for an evil child has begun the trouble must decide to confess consorting with the Devil, or die.

The expression 'witch hunt' has become familiar in recent years. In writing of Salem, Mr. Miller attempts no distant modern comparisons beyond stating timeless truths abut guilt and conscience and hysteria and bandwagon instincts. There are two highly memorable lines, both questions. 'Is the accuser always holy now?' the young husband cries. And 'Witchcraft is ipso facto invisible so who can testify against it?' asks the deputy-governor.

Mr. Miller has made important advances in the poetic quality of his writing in *The Crucible*. Its premiere last night was greeted with 19 curtain calls by a vociferous audience.

William Hawkins, *New York World Telegram*
and *The Sun*, 23 Jan. 1953

This is a play of enormous strength written with depth and intelligence: the characters declaim and behave as I assume they did in 1692; it is performed by a large and uniformly expert cast, the direction of Jed Harris is forceful and sympathetic.

Yet when I came away, with whistles and shouts of 'bravo!' still ringing in the house I had a lonely sense of unfulfillment. I was not greatly moved by anything that had happened.

There is no doubt of the validity of Miller's historical facts, give and take a little licence now and then, or the power of his writing, but it seemed to me that something was lacking in his choice of subject.

Fact or not, I found it constantly incredible that four malicious maidens in Salem 1692 could have corrupted the courts and brought about the horror, and execution of so many obviously innocent folk.

Okay, it happened. But it is so far beyond our present concepts of Justice and plausible behaviour that I never felt myself part of the proceedings. I never really believed the little monsters that set off the fuse, or that they could make their case stick with the Deputy-Governor of Massachusetts.

In *Death of a Salesman* Mr. Miller was writing about people he knew, that we all know, and thus established himself as one of our gifted young playwrights. *The Crucible* reveals the same high talent for dialogue, for a well rounded scene: I only wish he'd written it around people more understandable.

John McClain, *Journal American*, 23 Jan. 1953

Arthur Miller's expectantly awaited drama about witch-hunting in Salem, Mass., in the year 1692, was presented at the Martin Beck Theatre last evening by Kermit Bloomgarden. It is a stunning production, splendidly acted and strongly written.

However, those who may have expected Miller, an admitted liberal, to make a political parable of this play — as he did with Ibsen's *An*

Enemy of the People — will have to read into *The Crucible* their own implications, for the piece is just what it sets out to be; a tragic drama about the historic Puritan purge of witchcraft. It is, as it ends, the story of an upright man who finds within himself the courage to be hanged rather than to confess a guilt he does not own.

John Chapman, *Daily News*, 23 Jan. 1957

In *The Crucible*, Arthur Miller has penned a rip-roaring melodrama about the historic witch trials in Salem, Mass. He has designed a script for actors to act on a stage, rather than for pedants to read in a library. And that's what all good playwrights should aim to do.

Miller has etched *The Crucible* with broad strokes. Sometimes the dialogue resorts to a sort of blank verse, and at others to colloquial speech. But the two blend admirably. And he has developed robust situations on which to drape the wordage.

Robert Coleman, *Daily Mirror*, 23 Jan. 1953

Arthur Miller is a problem playwright in both senses of the word. As a man of independent thought, he is profoundly, angrily concerned with the immediate issues of our society — with the irresponsible pressures which are being brought to bear on free men, with the self-seeking which blinds whole segments of our civilization to justice, with the evasions and dishonesties into which cowardly men are daily slipping. And to his fiery editorializing he brings shrewd theatrical gifts: he knows how to make a point plain, how to give it bite in the illustration, how to make its caustic and cauterizing language ring out on the stage.

He is also an artist groping toward something more poetic than simple, savage journalism. He has not only the professional crusader's zeal for humanity, but the imaginative writer's feeling for it — how it really behaves, how it moves about a room, how it looks in its foolish as well as in its noble attitudes — and in his best play, *Death of a Salesman*, he was able to rise above the sermon and touch the spirit of some simple people.

In *The Crucible* which opened at the Martin Beck Thursday, he seems to me to be taking a step backward into mechanical parable, into the sort of play which lives not in the warmth of humbly observed human souls but in the ideological heat of polemic.

Make no mistake about it: there is fire in what Mr. Miller has to say, and there is a good bit of sting in his manner of saying it. He has for convenience's sake set his troubling narrative in the Salem of 1692. For reasons of their own, a quartet of exhibitionistic young women are hurling accusations of witchcraft at eminently respectable members of a well-meaning, but not entirely clear-headed society.

On the basis of hearsay — 'guilt by association with the devil' might be the phrase for it — a whole community of innocents are brought to trial and condemned to be hanged. As Mr. Miller pursues his very clear contemporary parallel, there are all sorts of relevant thrusts: the folk who do the final damage are not the lunatic fringe but the gullible pillars of society; the courts bog down into travesty in order to comply with the popular mood; slander becomes the weapon of opportunists ('Is the accuser always holy now?'): freedom is possible at the price of naming one's associates in crime: even the upright man is eventually tormented into going along with the mob to secure his own way of life, his own family.

Much of this — not all — is an accurate reading of our own turbulent age, and there are many times at the Martin Beck when one's intellectual sympathies go out to Mr. Miller and to his apt symbols anguishing on the stage. But it is the intellect which goes out, not the heart.

For Salem, and the people who live, love, fear and die in it, are really only conveniences to Mr. Miller, props to his thesis. He does not make them interesting in and for themselves, and you wind up analyzing them, checking their dilemmas against the latest headlines, rather than losing yourself in any rounded, deeply rewarding personalities. You stand back and think; you don't really share very much.

Walter Kerr, *New York Herald Tribune*, 23 Jan, 1953

Arthur Miller has written another powerful play. *The Crucible*, it is called, and it opened at the Martin Beck last evening in an equally powerful performance. Riffling back the pages of American history he has written the drama of the witch trials and hangings in Salem in 1692. Neither Mr. Miller nor his audiences are unaware of certain similarities between the perversions of justice then and today. . . .

Although *The Crucible* is a powerful drama it stands second to *Death of a Salesman* as a work of art. Mr. Miller has had more trouble with this one, perhaps because he is too conscious of its implications. The literary style is cruder. The early motivation is muffled in the uproar of the opening scene and the theme does not develop with the simple eloquence of *Death of a Salesman*.

It may be that Mr. Miller has tried to pack too much inside his drama, and that he has permitted himself to be concerned more with the technique of the witch hunt than with its humanity. For all its power generated on the surface, *The Crucible* is most moving in the simple quiet scenes between John Proctor and his wife. By the standards of *Death of a Salesman* there is too much excitement and not enough emotion in *The Crucible*. . . .

After the experience of *Death of a Salesman* we probably expect Mr. Miller to write a masterpiece every time. *The Crucible* is not of that stature and it lacks that universality. On a lower level of dramatic history with considerable pertinence for today, it is a powerful play and a genuine contribution to the season.

Brooks Atkinson, *New York Times*, 23 Jan. 1953

In scene after scene, it has the sort of ringing intensity that is fairly irresistible.

Emotionally, I think it is vastly successful. Where I found it a little disappointing in its final effectiveness is in Mr. Miller's inability to combine with it the kind of intellectual insight that was so notable in *Death of a Salesman* and made it one of the most distinguished dramas of the American theatre. To a certain extent, the author does delve into the causes and motives that created the background of the terrors which marked one of the darkest spots in our history. But he is chiefly concerned with what happened, rather than why, and this neglect sometimes gives his work a hint of superficiality.

While there is, to my mind, an unfortunate superficiality in *The Crucible*, the playwright deserves considerable credit for using implication, rather than too heavy an underlining to make his valuable points for today. There are, indeed, only a few moments when he doesn't let his sinister story speak for itself, and they are chiefly in the last act. But his characters tend to be dramatized points of view, or points of emotional hysteria, rather than the human beings that would have made them more striking in the theatre. Nevertheless, despite such weaknesses, there is much emotional fire and indignation which can approach the overwhelming. . . .

Richard Watts, Jr., *New York Post*, 23 Jan. 1953

I was disappointed in the reaction to *The Crucible* not only for the obvious reasons but because no critic seemed to sense what I was after. In 1953 McCarthyism probably helped to make it appear that the play was bounded on all sides by its arraignment of the witch hunt. The political trajectory was so clear — a fact of which I am a little proud — that what to me were equally if not more important elements were totally ignored. The new production, appearing in a warmer climate, may, I hope, flower, and these inner petals may make their appropriate appearance.

I was drawn to write *The Crucible* not merely as a response to McCarthyism. It is not any more an attempt to cure witch hunts than *Salesman* is a plea for the improvement of conditions for travelling men,

All My Sons a plea for better inspection of airplane parts, or *A View from the Bridge* an attack upon the Immigration Bureau. *The Crucible* is, internally, *Salesman*'s blood brother. It is examining the questions I was absorbed with before — the conflict between a man's raw deeds and his conception of himself; the question of whether conscience is in fact an organic part of the human being, and what happens when it is handed over not merely to the state or the mores of the time but to one's friend or wife. The big difference, I think, is that *The Crucible* sought to include a higher degree of consciousness than the earlier plays.

Arthur Miller, *New York Times*, 9 Mar. 1958

A Memory of Two Mondays

Play in one act.
First American production: Coronet Th., New York, 29 Sept. 1955
(dir. Martin Ritt; with Leo Penn as Bert, Van Heflin as Larry, and
J. Carrol Naish as Gus).
First British production: Playhouse, Nottingham, 29 Sept. 1958
(dir. Val May; with Terry Scully as Bert, Bryan Pringle as Larry, and
James Cossins as Gus).
*Published: A View from the Bridge: Two One-Act Plays by
Arthur Miller*, New York: Viking, 1955. In *Collected Plays*, Vol. 1,
New York: Viking, 1959; London: Cresset, 1950.

The play, part of a double bill with the one-act version of A View from the Bridge *when it was first presented in 1955, deals with life in an automobile parts warehouse. Bert is an eighteen-year-old who is working to earn enough money to pay his way through college. He is just passing through. The others, however, are trapped and we see something of the hermetic and suffocating nature of their lives.*

Memory is a plotless and leisurely play, an exploration of a mood, the mood of the thirties and the pathos of people forever locked into the working day. Some people paid me the inverse compliment of saying it had been written twenty years earlier and dredged out of the drawer, but, in fact, it was a reaching toward some kind of bedrock reality at a time, in 1954, when it seemed to me that the very notion of human relatedness had come apart.

It was McCarthy's time, when even the most remote conception of human solidarity was either under terrific attack or forgotten altogether. *A Memory of Two Mondays*, however lyrical and even nostalgic, was the evocation of a countervailing idea, the idea, quite simply, of 'other people', of sympathy for others, and finally of what I believed must come again lest we lose our humanity — a sense of sharing a common fate even as one escaped from it.

Arthur Miller, *New York Times*, 15 Aug. 1965

A Memory of Two Mondays is about several things. It is about mortality, first, in that the young man caught in the warehouse cannot understand what point there can be, beyond habit and necessity, for men to live this way. He is too young to find out, but it is hoped that the audience will glimpse one answer. It is that men live this way because they must serve an industrial apparatus which feeds them in body and leaves them to find sustenance for their souls as they may.

This play is a mortal romance. It expresses a preoccupation with the facts that everything we do in this fragmented world is so quickly wiped away and the goals, when won, are so disappointing. It is also the beginning of a further search and it lays the basis for a search. For it points the different roads people do take who are caught in warehouses, and in this play the warehouse is our world — a world in which things are endlessly sent and endlessly received; only time never comes back.

It is an abstract realism in form. It is in one act because I have chosen to say precisely enough about each character to form the image which drove me to write the play — enough and no more.

Arthur Miller, Introduction to *A View From the Bridge*

A View from the Bridge

(One-act version)
First American production: Coronet Th., New York, 29 Sept. 1955
(dir. Martin Ritt; with Van Heflin as Eddie, J. Carrol Naish as Alfieri, and Gloria Marlowe as Catherine).
Published: A View from the Bridge: Two One-Act Plays by Arthur Miller, New York: Viking, 1955.

(Two-act version)
First American production: Sheridan Square Playhouse, 28 Jan. 1965
(dir. Viv Grosband).
First London production: Comedy Th., London, 11 Oct. 1956
(dir. Peter Brook; with Anthony Quayle as Eddie, Michael Gwynn as

Alfieri, and Mary Ure and Megs Jenkins as Beatrice).
Revivals: Cottesloe Th., London, Feb. 1987 (dir. Alan Ayckbourn; with
    Michael Gambon as Eddie).
Published: New York: Dramatists Play Service, 1957. Harmondsworth:
    Penguin, 1961. In *Collected Plays*, Vol. 1, New York: Viking 1957;
    London, Cresset, 1958.
Film version: Paramount, 1961

---

*This play exists both in a one-act and a two-act form, the former
being in verse, the latter in prose. It concerns the growing and
confused love of Eddie Carbone for his niece, Catherine, a love
which he cannot acknowledge but which breeds a destructive
jealousy. This leads him to a profound suspicion of Rodolpho
who is drawn to Catherine and who, together with his brother,
Marco, is an illegal immigrant. Increasingly deranged, he
informs the immigration officials of their presence and is sub-
sequently challenged and killed by Marco. The story is told by a
lawyer-narrator, Alfieri.*

A *View from the Bridge* concerns present-day life in a colony of Italian-
American longshoremen on the Brooklyn waterfront. Although it is
vibrant with characters, this is no slice-of-life essay; it is a tragedy in the
classic form, and I think it is a modern classic. What happens in it
simply has to happen, and this is the inevitability of true tragedy. In it,
Van Heflin gives a magnificent performance as a longshoreman who,
though his mind is limited and he cannot find words for his thoughts, is
an admirable man. He is popular, kind, loyal, loving and generous.

This is an intensely absorbing drama, sure of itself every step of the
way. It makes no false moves, wastes no time and has the beauty that
comes from directness and simplicity. Some of the language in both the
Miller works is rough or bawdy, but it is true and it belongs and is not
there for shoddy sensationalism.

Arthur Miller has come a long way in our theatre, and he will go
much farther, for his mind is a mind that won't stay still.

John Chapman, *New York Daily News*, 30 Sept. 1955

No writer in the theatre understands better how to combine the poverty-
stricken imagery, the broken rhythms and mindless repetitions, and the
interminable clichés of illiterate speech into something that has a certain
harsh and grotesque eloquence. This is especially true of Eddie when he

is desperately trying to hide his guilt, both from himself and from a perceptive lawyer, under cover of a gathering fury of lies and contradictions, but it is apparent in the other characters, too, as they are drawn deeper and deeper into the nightmare he has created for them.

Altogether, when Mr. Miller is writing directly about the people involved in his action, his command of the idiom is nearly perfect and his treatment of dramatic incident is beyond criticism. In fact, the only complaint that I have to make of the whole offering is against a sort of extra and, in my opinion, distractingly literary touch that has been provided in the shape of the lawyer. This man not only fills in the gaps in the narrative but also points out its similarity in mood and design to classic Greek tragedy. He is a fairly rococo conversationalist, and it was my feeling that he served merely to bring a superfluous and rather pretentious air of classroom erudition to an otherwise admirably forthright play. I don't think it is too flattering to say that *A View from the Bridge* has no need of this kind of genteel embroidery.

Walcot Gibbs, *New Yorker*, 8 Oct. 1955

A View from the Bridge is in one act because, quite simply, I did not know how to pull a curtain down anywhere before its end. While writing it, I kept looking for an act curtain, a point of pause, but none ever developed. Actually it is practically a full-length play in number of pages, needing only the addition of a little material to make it obvious as such.

This play falls into a single act, also, because I saw the characters purely in terms of their action and because they are a kind of people who, when inactive, have no new significant definition as people. I use the word 'significant' because I am tired of documentation which, while perfectly apt and evidently reasonable, does not add anything to our comprehension of the tale's essence. In so writing, I have made the assumption that the audience is like me and would like to see, for once, a fine, high, always visible arc of forces moving in full view to a single explosion.

Arthur Miller, Introduction, *A View from the Bridge*

About a year later in London new conditions created new solutions. As a consequence of not having to work at making the play seem as factual, as bare as I had conceived it, I felt now that it could afford to include elements of simple human motivation which I had rigorously excluded before — specifically, the viewpoint of Eddie's wife, and *her* dilemma in relation to him. This, in fact, accounts for almost all the added material which made it necessary to break the play in the middle for an intermission. In other words, once Eddie had been placed squarely in his social context, among his people, the mythlike feeling of the story emerged of itself, and he could be made more human and less a figure, a force. It thus seemed quite in keeping that certain details of realism should be allowed; a Christmas tree and decorations in the living room, for one, and a realistic make-up, which had been avoided in New York, where the actor was always much cleaner than a longshoreman ever is. In a word, the nature of the British actor and of the production there made it possible to concentrate more upon realistic characterization while the universality of Eddie's type was strengthened at the same time.

In general, then, I think it can be said that by the addition of significant psychological and behavioral detail the play became not only more human, warmer and less remote, but also a clearer statement. Eddie is still not a man to weep over; the play does not attempt to swamp an audience in tears. But it is more possible now to relate his actions to our own and thus to understand ourselves a little better not only as isolated psychological entities, but as we connect to our fellows and our long past together.

Arthur Miller, *A View from the Bridge*,
(New York: Viking, Compass Edition, 1960), p. v-x

. . . It was more than a decade before I finally glimpsed something of myself in this play, when I saw Robert Duvall, a young actor I had never heard of until then, in Ulu Grosbard's powerful off-Broadway revival. As I watched Duvall, the most unimaginable of incarnations came through to me from his Eddie Carbone — I suddenly saw my father's adoration of my sister, and through his emotion, my own. When I wrote the play, I was moving through psychological country strange to me, ugly and forbidding. Yet something in me kept to the challenge to push on until a part of the truth of my nature unfolded itself in a scene, a word, a thought dropping onto my paper.

Arthur Miller, *Timebends*

After the Fall

Play in two acts.
First American production: ANTA — Washington Square Th.,
   New York, 23 Jan. 1964 (dir. Elia Kazan; with Jason Robards, Jr.,
   as Quentin and Barbara Loden as Maggie).
First British production: Belgrade Th., Coventry, 31 Oct. 1967

(dir. Leonard Schach; with Leon Gluckmann as Quentin,
Erica Rogers as Maggie).

Published: Saturday Evening Post, 1 Feb. 1964, p. 32-59.
New York: Viking, 1964. London: Secker and Warburg, 1965. In
Collected Plays, Vol. 2, New York: Viking 1981; London: Secker
and Warburg, 1981.

*Quentin, a successful lawyer, about to marry for the third time,
feels the need to examine the failure of his earlier marriages.
This, in turn, leads him to an exploration of betrayal in private
and public life. The central realities and metaphors become the
concentration camp and the House Un-American Activities
Committee. But these are seen as simply logical projections of a
flaw in the human psyche. Regarded at the time of its first
production as Miller's response to the failure of his relationship
with Marilyn Monroe, it was in fact an attempt to come to terms
with history no less than with personal concerns.*

In the last half of *After the Fall*, the playwright is mostly concerned
with a girl called Maggie, who bears an acute resemblance to
Marilyn Monroe, to whom Mr. Miller was once married. I don't know
about the ethics of bringing one's very recent marital life into public
view in infinite detail, but it is during these scenes that Mr. Miller builds
up a real head of dramatic steam, and somehow he makes Maggie a
figure well worth our pity, despite the fact that she has no more
conception of accepted morality than a cat, is drunk a lot of the time, and
can be shrill and abusive when she doesn't get her way.

John McCarten, *New Yorker*, Feb. 1964

We have seen the manner of all this often enough – the arena auditorium around the descending levels of the stage; bare, bathed in light,
which we are left to furnish for ourselves. It is the matter of
Arthur Miller's untimely apologia for the breaking of his marriage to
Marilyn Monroe that is finally arresting — an apologia which ends, not
for all its sordid detail, in putting Miller in the clear, but in becoming the
apologia for that poor radiant lost lady, his dead *seconde*, in the way that
a self-righteous politician animadverting against one who is fallible, by
overstating his case, angles our sympathies to the culprit. Was
Marilyn Monroe (for we can dismiss the dramatist's half-hearted
disguise of naming our anti-heroine Maggie) the culprit of the broken

marriage or the victim? That the question should be dramatized so soon
after her death by the man she married may be — is — in hideously bad
and bitter taste. But Miller, writing sparely at all times and superbly for
her, has at the heart of his play one speech that goes to the root of the
matter: it is in the second act and is spoken by the spokesman husband,
for the play takes place in his mind:

*You ever felt you once saw yourself — absolutely true? I may have
dreamed it, but I swear, I felt that somewhere along the line — with
Maggie, I think — for one split second I saw my life; what I had done,
what had been done to me, and even what I ought to do. And that vision
sometimes hangs behind my head, blind now, bleached out like the
moon in the morning; and if I could only let in some necessary darkness
it should shine again.*

This speech, then, is Miller the human being's answer to the accusation
that he has done Marilyn Monroe dirt; Miller the dramatist's answer
may be that he has, with the help of a clever actress, Barbara Loden,
shown us Marilyn Monroe in the round. And the play itself between the
lines proves clearly that life was the architect of Monroe's death. Was it
Shaw who said that what can be read between the lines of a play is the
only thing worth reading? To recreate a figure as innocent, as truthful, as
human, as trusting, as generous, as intellectually inadequate, as striving,
as shrill, as sensual, as hurt, as ruined, as disintegrating, as Marilyn, is to
fulfil the function of a playwright. Paint we a desolation, wrote Keats.
After the Fall has done just that.

Caryl Brahms, *The Spectator*, 14 Feb. 1964

Accepting one's life — at least in the context of *After the Fall* — is
more complicated than simply recognizing that any relationship implies
responsibilities on both sides. The guilt that Quentin assumes is
something very like original sin — an acceptance that he, of all men, are
evil or have evil in them, the capacity to kill. This idea is presented in
several ways in the play. Verbally, in Quentin's statements about his
failure to grieve for his dead — for Lou, for his mother, for Maggie.
Visually, in the scene in which he begins to strangle Maggie and finds
himself strangling his mother. Metaphorically, in the concentration camp
tower that broods over the whole play. This is the element of the play
that is most difficult to take, but it is a necessary part of the idea Miller
has imposed on his work. Near the end, Quentin turns toward the tower
and says, 'My brothers died here . . .' and then, looking down at Maggie
lying at his feet, adds, 'but my brothers built this place'. What is finally
being said in *After the Fall* is not that Quentin's life shows him capable

of cruelty, of murder even, but that he must accept his complicity in all the evil in the world. Holga, who carries the messages for Miller, says, '. . . no one they didn't kill can be innocent again.'

Gerald Weales, 'Arthur Miller in the 1960s' in
Arthur Miller, New Perspectives,
ed. Robert A. Martin

This play is not 'about' something; hopefully, it is something. And primarily it is a way of looking at man and his human nature as the only source of the violence which has come closer and closer to destroying the race. It is a view which does not look toward social or political ideas as the creators of violence, but into the nature of the human being himself. It should be clear now that no people or political system has a monopoly on violence. It is also clear that the one common denominator in all violent acts is the human being.

This play, then, is a trial; the trial of a man by his own conscience, his own values, his own deeds. The 'Listener', who to some will be a psychoanalyst, to others God, is Quentin himself turned at the edge of the abyss to look at his experience, his nature and his time in order to bring to light, to seize and — innocent no more — to forever guard against his own complicity with Cain, and the world's.

Arthur Miller, *Saturday Evening Post*,
1 Feb. 1964

I began to search for a form that would unearth the dynamics of denial itself, which seemed to me the massive lie of our time — while America, as I could not yet know, was preparing to fight a war in Vietnam and methodically deny it was a war and proceed to deny the men who fought the war the simple dignity of soldiers. I saw American culture, the most unfettered on earth, as the culture of denial; even as the drug, in expanding the mind, denied that it was destroying the mind, and the new freedom of sexuality denied that it was dissolving the compassionate self-restraint that made any human relationship conceivable over time. Costume and fashion allowed the stockholder's mind to deny the wearer of worker's jeans and secondhand clothes, whose free-flowing hair denied personal uninvolvement masquerading as liberated sensibility.

Inevitably the form of the new play was that of a confession, since the main character's quest for a connection to his own life was the issue, his conquest of denial the path into himself. It seemed neither more nor less autobiographical than anything else I had written for the stage. From the play I had abandoned a decade before, about a group of researchers suborned by a pharmaceuticals magnate, the figure of Lorraine emerged as the seeming truth-bearer of sensuality, contrasted with the constricted, mind-bound hero who looks to her for the revival of his life as she more and more comes to stand for the catlike authenticity of force of nature.

One learns to listen to what a developing play is trying to say. The theme of survivor guilt was emerging from the gargantuan manuscript.

It was after returning from Germany that I began to feel committed to the new play, possibly because its theme — the paradox of denial — seemed so eminently the theme of Germany, and Germany's idealistically denied brutality emblematic of the human dilemma in our time.

Looking back, I could see that in disconnecting the fictional character from any real person I was blinding myself to the obvious, but blame was certainly no part of the play; the very point of it all was that Maggie might be saved if she could cease to blame, either herself or others, and begin to see that like everyone else she had essentially made her own life, an awesome fact toward which one had to feel humility and wonder rather than such total remorse as was implied in her denial of any decisive part in her calamity. In this sense, innocence kills. But as I would shortly discover, it reigns, as it doubtless will forever.

I had not begun with the idea that Maggie would die but that she and Quentin would part, a stronger ending in that it would prevent the audience from disposing of the tale with comforting death. But as the character formed, she seemed more inescapably fated, and I could feel the bending of that arc toward death. And this also separated her in my mind from Marilyn, who as far as I knew was busy making films again. . . . As I was coming to the end of the writing of *After the Fall*, the horrifying news came that Marilyn had died, apparently of an overdose of sleeping pills.

Arthur Miller, Timebends

Incident at Vichy

Play in one act.
First American production: ANTA — Washington Square Th.,
 3 Dec. 1964 (dir. Harold Clurman; with David Wayne as Von Berg,
 and Joseph Wiseman as Leduc).
First British production: Theatre Royal, Brighton, 10 Jan. 1966
 (dir. Peter Wood; with Alec Guiness as Von Berg, and
 Anthony Quayle as Leduc).
Published: New York: Viking, 1965. London: Secker and Warburg,
 1966. In *Collected Plays*, Vol. 2, New York: Viking 1981; London:
 Secker and Warburg, 1981.

Set in Vichy France in 1942, the play concerns a group of people awaiting interrogation by the Germans. Some are to be released, others are to be sent on to a fate which they suspect and we know. Those to be released are given a special pass and the climax of the play comes as an Austrian Prince, von Berg, hands his pass to a doctor, Leduc, thus sacrificing his own life for another.

Arthur Miller, having apparently emerged from his dark period of bitter introspection, has turned to a short but intense drama of Occupied France in *Incident at Vichy*. Presented last night as the Lincoln Center Repertory Company's second offering of the season at its downtown headquarters below Washington Square, it is a kind of suspense thriller with moral overtones, and, while it is hardly one of his major works, it is continuously absorbing and indicates that he is getting back into his stride as a playwright of ideas.

Richard Watts, Jr., New York Post, 4 Dec. 1964

. . . While it is impossible to disagree with his thesis (which has been enunciated many times before) that any hatred in our hearts adds to the guilt we must feel at the consequences of all hatred, I don't think he has set forth his proposition with any dramatic flair, and his dialogue on occasion sounded to me as stilted as a bad interpretation of a language the interpreter is not entirely familiar with.

John McCarten, New Yorker, 12 Dec. 1964

The Price

Play in two acts.
First American production: Morosco Th., New York, 7 Feb. 1968
(dir. Ulu Grosbard; with Pat Hingle as Victor, Kate Reid as Esther,
Harold Gary as Gregory Solomon, and Arthur Kennedy as Walter).
First British production: Duke of York's Th., London, 4 Mar. 1969
(dir. Arthur Miller; with Albert Salmi as Victor, Kate Reid as Esther,
Harold Gary as Gregory Solomon, and Shepperd Strudwich
as Walter).
Published: New York: Viking, 1968. London: Secker and Warburg,
1968. In *Collected Plays*, Vol. 2, New York: Viking, 1981;
London: Secker and Warburg, 1981.

The Price *concerns two brothers, Victor and Walter, who meet after a separation of many years, in order to discuss the disposal of their father's property. The stage is piled high with furniture which they proceed to sell to a secondhand dealer called Solomon, elderly, ironic, humane. In the course of the play we learn of the background of the two brothers. One, Victor, is a policeman who had apparently sacrificed his chance to succeed in life in order to help his aging father. The other, Walter, has become a wealthy surgeon. But this comfortable contrast cannot be sustained and the process of the play slowly uncovers the self-deceits and fallibilities of all the characters. Besides much else this is a play which is notable for its humour, Solomon being a creation of great comic vitality.*

Arthur Miller's *The Price* (Morosco) is a stunning example of a difficult and often unproductive form of theatre. A little less adroitness on Miller's part, a slight shift in emphasis, a small let down in the sustained excellence of the performances, and this might easily have been a dramatically sterile talk session.

As it is, he has put two brothers and one of their wives in an attic of old furniture and let them storm the past — compellingly — with the anxious, rueful probing for which he is famous.

But if the play steeps itself in the past it is, of course, to elucidate the present, or at least to see enough of it to make meaningful the turmoil and flailing that ensue. . . .

Alan N. Bunce, *Christian Science Monitor*, 12 Feb. 1968

Miller opened a beautifully intelligent new play called *The Price*, about two brothers who are pinned in positions of flight from their own histories that are as fruitless as the movements of the men at Pompeii.

The play is virtually eventless, in the usual sense. its occurrences are in the brothers' understanding of the past, and of the cost of actions that they took long ago. It is thus obdurately at odds with anything else in the New York theatre, where the expression of a cool and kinless ethic about writing off last weeks's bungle as swiftly and indifferently as possible, seems to be a modish obligation that is equally binding on Broadway or off it.

Like *All My Sons* and *Death of a Salesman*, the new play follows a filament that leads way back into the past. Long ago, years before the curtain went up, the brothers made their choice of who to be. One of them became the sacrificial slogger who went into the police force and gave up a chance of science to support his father in the Depression. The other behaved in the style of the opportunist bright-boy, looking after himself, with the very Western justification of making a success of it. No one can write more harrowingly than Arthur Miller of a man's fanatic clutch on his self-assigned part. One of the energizing things about *The Price*, like all Miller's work, is his insistence in a very determinist society that we are the authors of our lives.

The Price isn't a conventionally theatrical evening. Miller has always been drawn to the theatre as a king of testimony. His characters are there not to combust, or whatever the current audience kicks come from, but to give evidence of their lives. The accounts they give of themselves in this play are often marvellously written, desperate, and sometimes very funny. . . . There are lines in the play that are going to stay in the public consciousness as did 'Attention must be paid' from *Death of a Salesman*; for instance, Franz's aching 'It's impossible to know what's important.'

People have theorized for ages about the death of heroic drama now that there are no respected kings or emperors to write about. And in the meantime Miller goes on making these lumbering, plaguing heroes out of policemen and salesmen. Maybe the reason he can do it is that, for him, heroism lies in the scale of a man's sense of the possibility of controlling his own life.

Penelope Gilliatt, *The Observer*, 11 Feb. 1968

I was impressed by Miller's intermittent insights ('we invent ourselves to wipe out what we know') and moved by the play's central dilemma: 'who's to take care of the helpless old father?' Such a theme, concerned as it is with retesting the boundaries of personal obligation, has seemed to many merely old-fashioned. In terms of current taste it is, but when that shifts, as it must, Miller's subtle inquiries will be more fully appreciated.

Martin Duberman, *Partisan Review*, Summer 1968

Arthur Miller in *The Price* has written a museum piece of a play to match the set. In form, substance and attitude, his newest drama is vintage 1930s. Always inclined to use the theatre as a preacher's pulpit, Miller sermonizes on his favourite themes: guilt, responsibility, and the way a man's identity is forged or warped by society's image of what he is or what he should be. In structure, though not in content, the central situation — the sibling rivalry of two brothers and their relationship to their father — somewhat resembles Miller's earlier successes, *All My Sons* and *Death of a Salesman*.

Time, 16 Feb. 1968

The Price is a play about real people, real issues and, above all, real illusions. . . . There is warmth in the play and also the chill that can emanate from exposed self-delusion. And parts of it are marvellously funny. . . .

What Mr. Miller is saying is that fine motives are often self-delusion, and although praiseworthy in themselves hold no patent of ultimate truth. . . .

The Price is a first-rate evening of theatre and an appropriate one in which to welcome Mr. Miller back to the full exercise of his talents.

Richard P. Cooke, *Wall Street Journal*, 9 Feb. 1968

The Price was in part an exorcism of this paralyzing vision of repetition. Two brothers meet again after an angry breakup many years before; the time has come to divide the family's possessions after the father's death. Grown men now, they think they have achieved the indifference to the betrayals of the past that maturity confers. But it all comes back; the old angry symbols evoke the old emotions of injustice, and they part unreconciled.

Despite my wishes I could not tamper with something the play and life seemed to be telling me, that we were doomed to perpetuate our illusions because truth was too terrible to face. At the end of the play Gregory Solomon, the eighty-nine-year-old used furniture dealer, is left with the family's possessions, which he has purchased from the brothers; he finds an old laughing record and, listening to it, starts laughing uncontrollably, nostalgically, brutally, having come closest to acceptance rather than denial of the deforming betrayals of time.

Arthur Miller, *Timebends*

Fame *and* The Reason Why

First American production: New Theater Workshop, New York, 1970 (with Eli Wallach and Anne Jackson).

The Creation of the World and Other Business

Play in three acts.
First American production: Shubert Th., New York, 30 Nov. 1972 (dir. Gerald Freedman; with Bob Dishy as Adam, Stephen Elliott as God and Zoe Caldwell as Eve).

First British production: Nicolson Square Th., Edinburgh
   (an Edinburgh Festival 'fringe' production), 17 Aug. 1974.
Published: New York: Viking, 1973. In *Collected Plays*, Vol. 2,
   New York: Viking, 1981; London: Secker and Warburg, 1981.

This work dramatizes the story of Adam and Eve to the moment in which Abel is slain by Cain.

By taking on the Book of Genesis as his starting point, Arthur Miller has tackled quite an ambitious subject for himself, and I'm sorry to say I can't believe he has carried it off successfully. His *The Creation of the World and Other Business*, which opened last night at the Shubert Theatre, has imagination and an unexpected vein of humour, and it starts out with a good first act. But by the end it seems to me to have become both confused and confusing.

A year or so ago, Pierre Boullez, the French novelist, wrote a charming little fantasy in which Eve upset God's designs for the world by stubbornly refusing to eat the apple. I wouldn't think of suggesting that Mr. Miller should have dramatized the Boullez story, but at least it had freshness and a good ironical point, while *Creation of the World* appeared to me uncertain of the viewpoint it was driving at and far from clear about its aim. It is an intelligent and inventive comedy of ideas but not a very satisfying one.

Richard Watts, *New York Post*, 1 Dec. 1972

Musing tiredly, and according to Genesis, on the wonder and mystery of man and his beginnings, Arthur Miller has wrought a play devoid of wonder, mystery or even the satisfying caress of fancy. In three acts, it is called *The Creation of the World and Other Business*, and it opened last night at the Shubert.

Uncertain in its approach, it tries to be both playful and serious-minded, failing in both instances. Its jesting is awkward and heavy-handed, its statements are preachy, and the writing, taken as a whole, is surprisingly flat and mechanical. If this is how we began, we shall all end in apathy.

In trying to unravel an eternal mystery, or at least shed some interesting light on it, the author has become so perplexed and perplexing that he can offer no solace other than the lame one that, well, at least Adam and Eve have each other. As the final curtain falls, even they don't appear too satisfied with the conclusion.

Douglas Watt, *New York Daily News*, 1 Dec. 1972

Like *The Price*, written in the sixties during the war, *Creation*, reconsidering Genesis, was essentially the fratricidal enigma, but seen now as a given of man's nature. In the setting of the original family, shorn of societal influence, the play seeks first principles; the competition between brothers for a mother's — and therefore God's — love is discovered with amazed perplexity for the first time. The purely loving and practical Adam and Eve, looking down in disbelief at the murdered Abel and the unrepentant Cain, can only fear for their lives under a god who not only permits such monstrous acts but has apparently designed mankind so as to perpetuate them. In this play the catastrophe is in man's primal nature; his brotherhood is where he first tastes the murder of his own kind. Against that ticking bomb within us the defence, if there is a defence, is hardly more than Adam's imprecation to his wife and remaining son — to an Eve filled with hatred for a defiant Cain; 'Ask her pardon! Cain, we are surrounded by the beasts! And God's not coming anymore! Boy, we are all that's left responsible — ask her pardon!' Cain, smiling and justified, walks adamantly away into his exile, leaving his father to call after him on his darkening desert, 'Mercy!'. But Adam's outcry is also integral to man.

Arthur Miller, Timebends

Up from Paradise

A theatre piece spoken and sung.
First American production: Power Center for the Performing Arts, Ann Arbor, Michigan, 23 Apr. 1974 (dir. Arthur Miller; with Arthur Miller as narrator).

A musical version of The Creation of the World and Other Business.

The Archbishop's Ceiling

Play in two acts.
First American production: Eisenhower Th., John F. Kennedy Center for the Performing Arts, Washington DC, 30 Apr. 1977 (dir. Arvin Brown; with Tony Musante as Adrian, John Cullum as Sigmund, Bibi Anderson as Maya, Josef Sommer as Martin, Douglas Watson as Marcus, Bara-Christen Hansen as Irena).

Revised text: Bolton Th., Cleveland, 12 Oct. 1984 (dir. Jonathan Bolt;
    with Morgan Lund as Adrian, Lizbeth Mackay as Maya,
    John Buck Jr. as Marcus, Sharon Bicknell as Irena, and
    Thomas S. Olenlacz as Sigmund).
First British production: Theatre Royal, Bristol, 1 Apr. 1985.
First London production: The Pit, Barbican Centre, 29 Oct. 1986.
Published: London: Methuen, 1984.

*A group of writers are gathered in a room in eastern Europe, a
room which is part of what was once an Archbishop's palace. In
the ceiling there may or may not be concealed microphones.
Their possible presence turns them all into actors. One of them,
Sigmund, has just had his manuscript stolen by the security
forces. He has turned for help to a fellow writer, but perhaps
also an agent of government, Marcus. Marcus is a friend but in
such a world friendship has to be examined for its meaning.
Also in the room is Maya, once, it seems, Marcus's lover but
someone who cares for Sigmund and who was once lover to
another writer present in the room — Adrian, a successful
American novelist. All of them combine, for their different
reasons, to persuade Sigmund to leave the country. He refuses
because to leave is not only to surrender, it is to drain his life of
meaning. But to stay is also to pay a price.* The Archbishop's
Ceiling *is a play of genuine metaphysical seriousness, though it
is not without wit.*

Arthur Miller, like Tennessee Williams, has been crucified by American
critics for failing to live up to his own genius. My own feeling is that
any man who has written *Death of a Salesman* and *The Crucible*
deserves constant respect, and that late Miller is far more full of matter
than has been realized. A case in point is *The Archbishop's Ceiling*, first
seen in Washington in 1977 and now being given its European premiere
by the admirable Bristol Old Vic. It is not a breathless masterpiece, but
it grips one's attention and confronts Miller's favourite theme of
personal integrity.

Writing in post-Watergate America, Miller deals partly with the way
bugging devices theatricalize human behaviour. We are in the sitting
room of a former Archbishop's palace, in an East European capital: the
baroque ceiling, once a testament to divine power, now symbolizes the
god-like authority of the state since it may be clustered with mikes. The
crisis beneath it is real; it is also addressed to the unseen masters.

The central question is whether Sigmund, a dissident writer of inter-national stature, should defect. The novel on which he has been working for five years has been confiscated by the police and all around him are voices urging him to go.

Marcus, the flat occupant and the kind of state-sanctioned writer who floats round the world of international conferences, wants Sigmund out so that his colleagues can operate in safety. Adrian, a visiting American novelist, offers Sigmund the lure of Western freedom and campus celebrity. Maya, the ex-mistress of all three men, wants to protect Sigmund from trial and prosecution.

Miller loves wrestling with an ethical problem (he is the Brooklyn Ibsen); and the key question here, as Miller himself says, is whether the individual should strive for independence or operate as a creature of power within the prevailing structure. It is a good question; but also a somewhat loaded one. In the West you can be part of society and yet openly critical; in the Eastern bloc such luxuries are generally denied. That is what makes the central debate slightly artificial since Sigmund, if he stays, will still presumably be a victimized, *samizdat* figure.

But, to its credit, the play tackles big issues and never resorts to heroes and villains. Marcus, the equivocal writer who has sought some accommodation with the state, is presented by Miller as a sympathetic, rational figure rather than a party hack: Sigmund, on the other hand, is an amiable egotist rather more concerned with his own integrity than the fate of his colleagues. And Miller never lets you forget the tragic absurdity of carrying on one's private debates in front of an unseen audience with characters moving into the corridor when they have something urgent to say.

Miller himself, I think, is guilty of offering a Western-humanist answer to a specifically East European problem; but it remains a complex, gritty, intellectually teasing play.

Michael Billington, *The Guardian*,
19 Apr. 1985

Even if I hadn't looked in the programme of Arthur Miller's *The Archbishop's Ceiling* (Bristol Old Vic), I think I would have guessed that we were in central Europe. The place is cluttered with massive but faded furniture which was once expensive, though probably not so much as the incongruously gleaming modern bric-a-brac. The room suggests both stubborn defensiveness and cheeky extravagance.

This is the home of Marcus, a writer who'd spent six years in Stalinist jails. His talent has dried up but his other vital juices haven't; he lives lavishly in a fairly honourable defeat, with Maya, tough and beguiling, but is not above bringing home from his foreign travels the odd, well-stacked Scandinavian nymphet who seems part of his perks, like his well-stocked drinks cabinet and his natty clothes.

The house used to be an archbishop's palace, and the ceiling of the title is a baroque extravaganza that might have been painted by Rudesheimer the Younger or some such. What no one knows is whether the ceiling also contains a listening device. Is Marcus being bugged by the people's republic as well as by his sense of failure, and his decent yet bleak belief that the status quo, though barely bearable, is still preferable to the recent past?

Technically, the play is about Sigmund, a great writer who can neither bear nor understand compromise, and whom Marcus may or may not be able to save (or want to save) from his own ferocious and impetuous integrity. But Miller's real subject is authenticity. Who are we when we talk? And are we the same when we know someone is listening? . . . No other playwright has recalled so vividly for me that curious sensation, both humiliating and eerie, when one's perfectly ordinary conversation can feel as if it had been scripted by an uninspired scriptwriter.

Does all this sound gibberish to a British reader? We know that some phones are tapped, when they shouldn't be; but are we confident that it's a pointless thing to do because we always 'speak what we feel, not what we ought to say'? (Even Shakespeare knew something about this, you see.) Perhaps Miller's most interesting character is Adrian, the American novelist, whose motives for being here are as confused as his mind is honourable, and whose innocent bewilderment about nuances is, if anything, ennobled by his simple but unshakeable grasp of moral essentials.

It would have been easy for Miller, with his record as a victim of political crookery, to write a plague-on-both-your-houses type of play. But there's nothing self-righteous or complacent about this work; it is full of a giant and warm humanity, and the uncomfortable honesty of a man who is his own moral inquisitor.

John Peter, *Sunday Times*, 21 Apr. 1985

I saw it once before, in a good production, and was struck by its sheer moral intelligence: the force with which Miller is able to penetrate the murky world of Eastern Europe and its dangerous crossroads of art and politics, conscience and survival. Now, Nick Hamm's production deepens the sense of density, of three-dimensional solidity about both people and arguments.

Partly, I realize, it is simply a question of seeing it a second time and absorbing more. (This is a bit of a luxury, I know: how many theatregoers can afford to see the same play twice?) But it is also true that some plays give you all there is to them on first acquaintance. By contrast, *The Archbishop's Ceiling*, like certain thoughtful and reserved people, open up to you only gradually. Miller's first master was Ibsen, who left him a double inheritance. One is the sombre insistence that private morality will inevitably express itself in public action. The other is that relationships between people are subtle, complicated, elusive, and only partly understood by themselves; and that if you want to understand them you need to watch them attentively, and with a certain selfless humility.

And so, as you watch Adrian, the beady-eyed but helplessly honest American visitor (Roger Allam, welcome back) you gradually sense the special quality of American innocence abroad: confident, shrewd, but lacking the deviousness of people who are used to being defeated. As you watch Marcus the ageing writer (David de Keyser), you understand, item by item, the daily spiritual expenditure which, to someone essentially decent, is the cost of compromise.

And there's nothing starry-eyed either about Miller's writing: as you watch Sigmund, the dissident writer (John Shrapnel), you appreciate not only his courage but also his obduracy, his lack of control (he spends it all on his writing), and his terrible need for reassurance through persecution. If the ceiling of the title has a listening device in it, we sense it not only as a dark and malignant presence but also as a demanding divinity, the source of a helplessly masochistic religion.

The production reveals, too, an atmosphere of weary complicity which so often strikes Anglo-Saxons in their dealings with Eastern Europeans: that behind the self-assurance and the easy camaraderie there's another, secret language being spoken by experienced conspirators. You sense, too, the impatience of Eastern Europeans in the face of boisterous transatlantic innocence, as when Maya, Marcus's ex-wife (Jane Lapotaire), realizes that Adrian is excited, not so much by her as by seeing himself in a dangerous situation.

John Peter, *Sunday Times*,
2 Nov. 1986

The American Clock

Play in two acts.
First American production: previewed at Harold Clurman Th.,
    New York, but opened at Spoleto Festival's Dockside Th.,
    Charleston, South Carolina, 24 May 1980.
New York production: Biltmore Th., 20 Nov. 1980
    (dir. Vivian Matalon; with John Randolph as Moe,

Joan Copeland as Rose, and William Atherton as Lee).
First British production: Birmingham Repertory Th., 18 April 1983.
First London production: Cottesloe Th., 6 Aug. 1986.
Published: London: Methuen, 1983.

This play sets out to capture something of the mood and reality of Depression America. At its heart is the story of the Baum family — very close in some respects to Miller's own. They are middle class but quickly lose much of what they own. Meanwhile all of America is adjusting to a new reality and, through what amounts almost to a vaudeville style, he offers glimpses of America as it struggled through the thirties. We see dramatized moments which underscore the nature of rural and urban poverty. Linking these fragmentary scenes — which in some respects are deliberate pastiches of thirties' drama — are the songs which accompanied the bread lines and the soup kitchens.

The first thing to assert about Peter Wood's production for his own National Theatre group is that it reaffirms Miller's reputation at a stroke and suggests we may have to look at all his plays of the last decade or so much more carefully.

It is an ensemble event opening with the financier's 1929 recommendation to his shoeshine boy to sell up his stock. We zoom in on the Baum family, in which two cousins, Lee and Sydney, are shown respectively struggling to win a college place and write a hit tune. Our visitations to this family are almost phantasmagoric, outlines of what happens emerging amid a welter of Depression songs (Mr. Wood's biggest structural innovation) and a series of vignettes, reflective monologues and even an auction in Iowa at which the farm workers try to lynch a judge and buy back their land for a dollar.

You can see how that episode, and others, might seem awkward or obtrusive. But the scene is introduced by the company assembling in a straight line and singing a hymn.

The Baums are close relations of Miller's Loman family and Michael Bryant as Moe, the bleached and sorrowful salesman, and Sara Kestelman as Rose, his music-loving wife, gradually take hold of the play's emotional centre.

Lee, beautifully played by Neil Daglish, advances from bicycle-riding adolescence to would-be journalist, losing his political ideology in an attempt to seduce an attractive but earnest Superman cartoonist. In a complementary reversal of that scene, Lee's dental student friend

(Steven Law) reads Engels to a hooker (Marsha Hunt) intent only on removing his long johns.

The Baums are shown on the skids, Rose losing her grip as well as her piano, Moe shutting the door on his own son. The narrator, whom Barrie Ingham plays as increasingly wise and wheelchair-bound, draws some finger-wagging conclusions about the loss of opportunity in the age of corporate industry, the erosion of small enterprise and self-improvement. As a theme, this is wearing a bit thin.

On the other hand, Miller's aim is not just to memorialize old times but to suggest we can learn by celebrating them. He has often written about the underdog, but never in this way.

Michael Coveney, *Financial Times*, 7 Aug. 1986

The American Clock is a spellbinding theatrical event. It isn't really like Miller at all: it lacks the tight composition and the distilled moral indignation of his best-known work. It is a loosely built, episodic lament for the America of the Depression years in which Miller spent his adolescence: freewheeling, humorous, melancholy, and full of unsentimental sympathy for the men and women, brave and bigoted, garrulous and grasping, who went under or survived. It could be called Roosevelt's Children.

Wood's way with the text is free but never high-handed: he brings to it an inventive and irresistible theatricality which never obscures the hard edges of Miller's picture. Its pedigree is excellent. Theatrically, it's a treat.

John Peter, *Sunday Times*, 10 Aug. 1986

Elegy for a Lady

Play in one act.
First American production: in double-bill with *Some Kind of Love Story*, Long Wharf Th., New Haven, Nov. 1982
(dir. Miller; with Christine Lahti and Charles Cioffi).
Published: New York: Dramatists' Play Service, 1984
(acting edition). In *Two-Way Mirror*, London: Methuen, 1984.

A man enters a boutique supposedly to buy flowers for a dying woman. The proprietress responds, in so doing seemingly offering some insight into the life of the absent woman. But the piece is not naturalistic and it is impossible to be sure that there is such a person. Perhaps the man is a figment of her imagination or it may even be the other way round. It is a play about memory, about how we constitute the real, about how we invent the world which we inhabit.

Some Kind of Love Story

Play in one act.
First American production: in double-bill with *Elegy for a Lady*,
   Long Wharf Th., New Haven, Nov. 1982 (dir. Miller;
   with Christine Lahti and Charles Cioffi).
Published: New York: Dramatists' Play Service, 1984
   (acting edition). In *Two-Way Mirror*, London: Methuen, 1984

Tom O'Toole is a detective investigating a five year old murder for which a man is already serving a sentence. But a witness to the crime — Angela — hints at a different version of events. When she is questioned, however, she retreats into a series of alternative personalities or into catatonia. Detective and witness have been lovers and it is possible that the interrogations are little more than excuses for them to meet again. Certainly it is impossible to be sure that she has the information at which she hints or that the detective has no ulterior motive in seeking her out.

I Can't Remember Anything

Play in one act.
First American production: Lincoln Center, New York, January 1987.
Published: in *Danger! Memory*. London: Methuen, 1986,
   New York: Grove Press, 1987.

Leo and Leonora sit in a living room-kitchen discussing a past which seems to have drifted away from them as they occupy a present which itself is uncertain in its implications.

Clara

Play in one act.
First American production: Lincoln Centre, New York, Jan. 1987

An interrogation by a police lieutenant slowly elicits information about a murder victim and her assailant from her father. He is in a state of shock and his perception of events is externalized through character and through slide projectors.

Playing for Time

Play in two acts.
First American production: Studio Th., Washington D.C.,
    22 Sept. 1985.
Published: Chicago: Dramatic Publishing Company, 1985
    (acting edition).

Originally a television film, based on a book by Fania Fenelon,
Playing for Time *tells the story of the women's orchestra forced to play at the Auschwitz/Birkenau concentration camp during the Second World War. Its principal character is Fania Fenelon and the drama centres on her guilt, her pain and her growing need to find some way in which she can resist. But she is not alone. Of almost equal importance is the leader of the orchestra, Alma, who knows all too well that the central theme of their lives must be survival.*

Fania's survival is directly due to her musical ability which leads to her being chosen to join the all-women orchestra formed to entertain the German camp staff. Her moral dilemma is obvious and it is accentuated when the Camp Comandant praises her singing; 'It is a consolation that feeds the spirit. It strengthens us for this difficult work of ours.' Relief at her salvation is tempered by an evident distaste for the means by which that end is achieved. She plays on — playing for time — but courageously makes demands on her captors. Her initial consent she

57

makes conditional on Marianne's being allowed to join the orchestra too; she insists on telling the Commandant that her family name is not Fenelon but Goldstein; and she tries to secure privileges for the the other girls. Yet all these assertions of her independence alternate with more cautious, even obsequious, modes of address to her captors, and her insecure vulnerability is never masked. It comes as a shock to her to realize how the other internees regard her: 'I'm just not used to being hated like that.'

Even the other members of the orchestra are at times hostile to her, as on the occasion when she and Marianne are allowed to symbolize their half-Jewishness by removing half of the Star of David from their tunics. The quarrel that this provokes leads Fania to denounce the categories into which ideologies automatically force people: 'I am sick of it, sick of it, sick of it! I am a woman, not a tribe! And I am humiliated! That is all I know.' Throughout the play Miller contrasts Fania with Esther, who plays the drums, and whom in a stage direction he describes as 'a taut, militant Zionist'. Esther's declaration, 'I am only keeping myself for Jerusalem' has a smug fanaticism far less attractive than Fania's perplexed uncertainty. Fania sews back the half of the Star that she has removed but she does so with anger and resentment, partly at herself for needing this display of solidarity. In the screen version, at a later point in the play, one of the Polish women tries to define why the prisoners respect Fania and share their confidences with her: 'You have no ideology. You're just satisfied to be a person.' The statement strikes a keynote that has reverberated throughout Miller's work, but not always with the peculiar resonance it acquires here.

Fania is also contrasted increasingly with Marianne. Captivity, deprivation and fear weaken the younger girl's character and she seeks self-preservation through prostituting herself to the Germans. Not only is her degeneration set against Fania's strength, her selfishness against Fania's altruism, but her conduct tacitly exemplifies a distinction that is always crucial to Miller: to have no ideology is not the same as to have no principles. There is in the play no overt Shavian debate on the moral issues involved, but neither is there any doubt as to the distinction Miller is drawing between Fania's choice and Marianne's.

Denis Welland,
Miller the Playwright

b: Radio Plays

The Pussycat and the Expert Plumber Who Was a Man

Published: in *One Hundred Non-Royalty Plays*, ed. William Koslenko.
  New York: Greenberg, 1941, p. 20-30.

A discussion between a talking cat and a plumber about the nature of the human animal with the cat assuming that people are most concerned with their public reputation and the plumber convinced that the only true judge of integrity is the independent self.

William Ireland's Confession

Published: in *One Hundred Non-Royalty Plays*, p. 512-21.

The play concerns a forger of Shakespeare's manuscripts.

The Four Freedoms

Unpublished: Ms. in Library of Congress.

Grandpa and the Statue

Published: in *Radio Drama in Action*, ed. Erik Barnouw.
  New York: Farrar and Rinehart, 1945, p. 265-81.

The protagonist at first refuses to give money for the erection of the pedestal of the Statue of Liberty but eventually agrees to do so, thereby acknowledging a responsibility to the society in which he lives.

The Story of Gus

Published: in *Radio's Best Plays*, ed. Joseph Liss.
   New York: Greenberg 1947, p. 303-19.
Unproduced.

The story is a patriotic account of an individual in the wartime merchant marines.

The Guardsman

Adapted by Miller from the work by Ferenc Molnar.
Published: in *Theatre Guild on the Air*, ed. H. William Fitelson.
   New York: Rinehart, 1947, p. 69-97.

Three Men on a Horse

Adapted by Miller from the work by George Abbott and
   John C. Holm.
Published: in *Theatre Guild on the Air*, p. 207-38.

c: Television Plays

Fame

First transmitted: NBC, 30 Nov. 1978 (with Richard Benjamin as
   Meyer Shine, José Ferrer as Francesco, Shra Donesa as Lusic, and
   Linda Hunt as Mona).

In November 1978 American television screened a play by Miller entitled *Fame*. Although announced as 'a new play', it is presumably related to his piece of the same name that was presented unobtrusively in New York in 1970. Its relation to the 1966 short story, 'Fame', however, is minimal. The television piece concerns an American dramatist, Meyer Shine, coming to terms with the fame that his three successful plays have brought him.

Dennis Welland, *Miller the Playwright*

Playing for Time

First transmitted: CBS, 30 Sept. 1980 (with Vanessa Redgrave as Fania Fenelon and Jane Alexander as Alma Rose).
Published: New York: Bantam Books, 1981. In *Collected Plays*, Vol. 2.

d: Films

The Hook

'A play for the screen'.
Unproduced and unpublished.

Written in 1951, this was to be a film about the New York waterfront centering on the figure of Marty who stands up to the corrupt union officials who are in league with the ship owners. Dismissed from his job, he runs a campaign which for a while unifies the dock workers, giving them a sense of their corporate strength. Miller was asked, in the context of the Korean War, to substitute communists for the gangster labour leaders. He refused and the film was never made.

Death of a Salesman

Columbia Pictures, 1952 (dir. Laszlo Bendek; with Frederic March as

Willy, Mildred Dunock as Linda, Kevin McCarthy as Biff, and
Cameron Mitchell as Happy).

Les Sorcieres

Films de France, 1957 (dir. Raymond Rouleau; screenplay by
Jean-Paul Sartre; with Yves Montand as John Proctor,
Simone Signoret as Elizabeth, and Mylene Demongeot as Abigail).

The Misfits

United Artists, 1961 (dir. John Huston; with Clark Gable,
Marilyn Monroe, Montgomery Clift, Thelma Riter and Eli Wallach).

*A film, starring Marilyn Monroe, Clark Gable and Montgomery
Clift, in which Roslyn, in Reno for a divorce, falls in love with
an aging cowboy called Gay who makes his living by capturing
wild horses and selling them to a manufacturer of dog food.
Eventually Roslyn persuades Gay and his companion Perce to
release them. The dream of genuine human relationships
conducted in a world uncorrupted by materialism is allowed one
more moment of life.*

e: Operas

The Crucible

Libretto by Bernard Stambler; music by Robert Ward.
First American production: New York City Center of Opera and Drama,
26 Oct. 1961.
Published: New York: Galaxy Music Corporation, 1961.

a: Novels

The Man Who Had All the Luck

Novel.
Unpublished.

Focus

Novel.
Published: New York: Reynal, 1945. London: Gollancz, 1949.
Harmondsworth: Penguin, 1978.

Lawrence Newman is a personnel executive for a New York company. Failing eyesight requires him to obtain spectacles which have the inadvertent effect of making him look Jewish. Immediately he begins to feel the impact of anti-semitism and in the face of a growing hostility his life begins to fall apart. Eventually he accepts the identity forced upon him and resists the prejudice which he encounters.

b: Short Stories

'It Takes a Thief'. *Collier's*, CXIX (8 Feb. 1947), p. 23, 75-6.
'Monte Saint Angelo'. *Harper's*, CCII (Mar. 1951), p. 39-47.
   Reprinted as 'Monte Sant' Angelo' in *I Don't Need You Any More*, short story collection.
'The Misfits'. *Esquire*, XLVIII (Oct. 1957), p. 158-66.
'I Don't Need You Any More'. *Esquire*, LII (Dec. 1959), p. 270-309.
'Please Don't Kill Anything'. *The Noble Savage*, No. 1 (Mar. 1960), p. 126-31. Reprinted in *Redbook*, CXVII (Oct. 1961), p. 48-9.
'The Prophecy'. *Esquire*, LVI (Dec. 1961), p. 268-87.

'Glimpse at a Jockey'. *The Noble Savage*, No. 5 (Oct. 1962),
  p. 138-40.
Jane's Blanket. New York: Collier-Macmillan, 1963.
'The Recognitions'. *Esquire*, LVI (July 1966), p. 76, 118. Appears as
  'Fame' in *I Don't Need You Any More*.
'A Search for a Future'. *The Saturday Evening Post*, CCXXXIX
  (13 Aug. 1966), p. 64-8, 70. Reprinted in *I Don't Need You Any
  More*.
I Don't Need You Any More (short story collection). New York: Viking,
  1967. Contains a 'Foreword: About Distances' by Miller; 'I Don't
  Need You Any More'; 'Monte Sant' Angelo'; 'Please Don't Kill
  Anything'; 'The Misfits'; 'Glimpse at a Jockey'; 'The
  Prophecy';'Fame'; 'Fitter's Night', and 'A Search for a Future'.
  London: Secker and Warburg, 1967.
'Kidnapped?'. *The Saturday Evening Post*, CCXLII (25 Jan. 1969),
  p. 40-2, 78-82.
'Rain in a Strange City'. *Travel and Leisure*, IV (Sept. 1974), p. 8
'Ham Sandwich'. *Boston University Journal*, XXIV, No. 2 (1976),
  p. 5–6.

c: Non-Fiction

Situation Normal. New York: Reynal and Hitchcock, 1944.
In Russia (with Inge Morath). New York: Viking, 1969.
  London: Secker and Warburg, 1969.
In the Country (with Inge Morath). New York: Viking, 1977.
  London: Secker and Warburg, 1977.
The Theatre Essays of Arthur Miller, ed. Robert A. Martin.
  New York: Viking, 1978. Harmondsworth: Penguin, 1978.
  London: Secker and Warburg, 1979.
Chinese Encounters (with Inge Morath). New York: Farrar,
  Straus and Giroux, 1979.
Salesman in Beijing (photographs by Inge Morath). New York:
  Viking, 1984. London: Methuen, 1984.

The very impulse to write, I think, springs from an inner chaos crying for order, for meaning, and that meaning must be discovered in the process of writing or the work lies dead as it is finished. To speak, therefore, of a play as though it were the objective work of a propagandist is an almost biological kind of nonsense, provided, of course, that it is a play, which is to say a work of art.

Introduction to the *Collected Plays*

Politics and Drama

A play cannot be equated with a political philosophy, at least not in the way a smaller number, by simple multiplication, can be assimilated into a larger. I do not believe that any work of art can help but be diminished by its adherence at any cost to a political programme, including its author's, and not for any other reason than that there is no political programme — any more than there is a theory of tragedy — which can encompass the complexities of real life. Doubtless an author's politics must be one element, and even an important one, in the germination of his art, but if it is art he has created it must by definition bend itself to his observation rather than to his opinions or even his hopes.

Introduction to the *Collected Plays*

Theatre

For myself, the theatre is above all else an instrument of passion. However important considerations of style and form have been to me, they are only means, tools to pry up the well-worn, 'inevitable' surfaces of experience behind which swarm the living thoughts and feelings whose expression is the essential purpose of art.

By whatever means it is accomplished, the prime business of a play is to arouse the passions of its audience so that by the route of passion may be opened up new relationships between a man and men, and between men and Man. Drama is akin to the other inventions of man in that it ought to help us to know more, and not merely to spend our feelings.

Introduction to the *Collected Plays*

The Theatre as Collective Experience

The whole notion of going into a theatre and sitting with a lot of other people and watching a spectacle, especially now when you can watch television or the movies with great convenience, tells me that, apart from the fact that it's a little more exciting to see a live actor on the stage, it's also exciting to sit next to human beings. I think people need that; they have to feel that when they laugh together there is a relatedness. They learn what's funny.

I think that the theatre does break down an unrelatedness in people — to a degree. It refreshes the spirit which now experiences the reactions of other people, if only through looking at a common spectacle.

Interviewed by J. Martine in *Critical Essays on Arthur Miller*

An Impatient Moralist

I had made no bones about being a rather impatient moralist, not even in interviews, where I was naive enough to confess that to me an amoral art was a contradiction and that an artist was obliged to point a way out if he thought he knew what it was. I had unknowingly picked up where my beloved Russians had left off, but without Tolstoy's and Dostoyevsky's privilege of a god whose unearthly resolutions, as in *Crime and Punishment*, one did not have to believe in reasonably but only sense to validate. I was striving toward a sensation of religious superreality that did not, however, depart the conditions of earth, a vision of avoidance of evil that would thrill even atheists and lead them 'upward', and perhaps even shame priest and rabbi into realizing how their 'spiritualizing' of raw life had made a trifle of religions. The more exactingly true a character or dilemma was, the more spiritualized it became.

Timebends

Realism

Realism, heightened or conventional, is neither more nor less an artifice, a species of poetic symbolization, than any other form. It is merely more familiar in this age. If it is used as a covering of safety against the evaluation of life it must be overthrown, and for that reason above all the rest. But neither poetry nor liberation can come merely from a rearrangement of the lights or from leaving the skeletons of the flats exposed instead of covered by painted cloths; nor can it come merely from the masking of the human face or the transformation of speech into rhythmic verse, or from the expunging of common details of life's apparencies. A new poem on the stage is a new concept of relationships between the one and the many and the many and history, and to create it requires greater attention, not less, to the inexorable, common, pervasive conditions of existence in this time and this hour. Otherwise only a new self-indulgence is created, and it will be left behind, however poetic its surface.

I have stood squarely in conventional realism; I have tried to expand it with an imposition of various forms in order to speak more directly, even more abruptly and nakedly of what has moved me behind the visible facades of life.

Introduction to the *Collected Plays*

The longer I dwelt on the whole spectacle, the more clear became the failure of the present age to find a universal moral sanction, and the power of realism's hold on our theatre was an aspect of this vacuum. For it began to appear that our inability to break more than the surfaces of realism reflected our inability — playwrights and audiences — to agree upon the pantheon of forces and values which must lie behind the realistic surfaces of life. In this light, realism, as a style, could seem to be a defence against the assertion of meaning. How strange a conclusion this is when one realizes that the same style seventy years ago was the prime instrument of those who sought to illuminate meaning in the theatre, who divested their plays of fancy talk and improbable locales and bizarre characters in order to bring 'life' onto the stage. And I wondered then what was true. Was it that we had come to fear the hard glare of life on the stage and under the guise of an aesthetic surfeited with realism were merely expressing our flight from reality? Or was our condemned realism only the counterfeit of the original, whose most powerful single impetus was to deal with man as a social animal? Any form can be drained of its informing purpose, can be used to convey, like the Tudor facades of college dormitories, the now vanished dignity and necessity of a former age in order to lend specious justification for a present hollowness. Was it realism that stood in the way of meaning or was it the counterfeit of realism?

Introduction to the *Collected Plays*

With *Streetcar*, Tennessee had printed a licence to speak at full throat, and it helped strengthen me as I turned to Willy Loman, a salesman always full of words, and better yet, a man who could never cease trying, like Adam, to name himself and the world's wonders. I had known all along that this play could not be encompassed by conventional realism, and for one integral reason: in Willy the past was as alive as what was happening at the moment, sometimes even crashing in to completely overwhelm his mind. I wanted precisely the same fluidity in the form, and now it was clear to me that this must be primarily verbal. The language would of course have to be recognizably his to begin with, but it seemed possible now to infiltrate it with a kind of superconsciousness. The play, after all, involved the attempts of his sons and his wife and Willy himself to understand what was killing him. And to understand meant to lift the experience into emergency speech of an unashamedly open kind rather than to proceed by the crabbed dramatic hints and pretexts of the 'natural.' If the structure had to mirror the psychology as directly as could be done, it was still a psychology hammered into its strange shape by society, the business life Willy had lived and believed in. The play could reflect what I had always sensed as the unbroken tissue that was man and society, a single unit rather than two.

Timebends

The Depression

I did not read many books in those days. The depression was my book. Years later I could put together what in those days were only feelings, sensations, impressions. There was the sense that everything had dried up. Some plague of invisible grasshoppers was eating money before you could get your hands on it. You had to be a PH.D. to get a job in Macy's. Lawyers were selling ties. Everybody was trying to sell something to everybody else. A past president of the Stock Exchange was sent to jail for misappropriating trust funds. They were looking for runaway financiers all over Europe and South America. Practically everything that had been said and done up to 1929 turned out to be a fake. It turns out that there had never been anybody in charge.

What the time gave me, I think now, was a sense of an invisible world. A reality had been secretly accumulating its climax according to its hidden laws to explode illusion at the proper time. In that sense 1929 was our Greek year. The gods had spoken, the gods, whose wisdom had been set aside or distorted by a civilization that was to go onward and upward on speculation, gambling, graft, and the dog eating the dog. Before the crash I thought 'Society' meant the rich people in the Social Register. After the crash it meant the constant visits of strange men who knocked on our door pleading for a chance to wash the windows, and some of them fainted on the back porch from hunger. In Brooklyn, New York. In the light of weekday afternoons.

There are a thousand things to say about that time but maybe one will be evocative enough. Until 1929 I thought things were pretty solid. Specifically, I thought — like most Americans — that somebody was in charge. I didn't know exactly who it was, but it was probably a businessman, and he was a realist, a no-nonsense fellow, practical, honest, responsible. In 1929 he jumped out of the window. It was bewildering.

Harper's, CCXVII (Aug. 1958), p. 35-43

Social Plays

To put it simply, even oversimply, a drama rises in stature and intensity in proportion to the weight of its application to all manner of men. It gains its weight as it deals with more and more of the whole man, not either his subjective or his social life alone, and the Greek was unable to conceive of man or anything else except as a whole. The modern playwright, at least in America, on the one hand is importuned by his most demanding audience to write importantly, while on the other he is asked not to bring onto the stage images of social function, lest he seem like a special pleader and therefore inartistic. I am not attempting a defence of the social dramas of the thirties, most of which were in fact special pleadings and further from a consideration of the whole man than much of the anti-social drama is. I am trying only to project a right conception of what social drama was and what it ought to be. It is, I think, the widest concept of drama available to us thus far.

The social drama, then — at least as I have always conceived it — is the drama of the whole man. It seeks to deal with his differences from other not *per se*, but toward the end that, if only through drama, we may know how much the same we are, for if we lose that knowledge we shall have nothing left at all. The social drama to me is only incidentally an arraignment of society. *A Streetcar Named Desire* is a social drama; so is *The Hairy Ape*, and so are practically all O'Neill's other plays. For they ultimately make moot, either weakly or with full power, the ancient question, how are we to live? And that question is in its Greek sense, its best and most humane sense, not merely a private query.

From the original edition of *A View from the Bridge*
(New York: Viking, 1955), p. 1-18

Social Drama

Ibsen was, like any writer of any value, a private man and was not simply a public speaker. But the purpose of the form was not self-indulgence but to express to his fellow citizens what his vision was. The same thing is true of the Greeks.

At Michigan, of course, we were in a moment of great social stress, when the virtues of being totally cut off from man and from society were non-existent. One didn't consider that — at least I didn't. Art had a purpose, which was communicative. And I fell heir, so to speak, to the notion of the dramatist being a sort of prophet. He was the leading edge of the audience. This was implicit in the whole notion of literature in the 1930s.

But, of course, it was also part of the Ibsen and Greek notion too. Aeschylus, on his tombstone, after all, doesn't speak of himself particularly as a writer, but as a defender of the state and the democracy against the Persians. That's how he wanted to be remembered. I'm sure that infiltrated into all his work too. It certainly did into the *Oresteia* and many other works as well.

I think that man is a social animal; there's no getting away from it. He's in society the way a fish is in the water, and the water is in the fish. I can't possibly disentangle them, and I think those plays indicate that. As a matter of fact, I've tried, I think, in the interest of truthfulness, to take as far as I can that awareness of my own in these dramas — because I'm under no illusions that people really invent themselves. They do to a degree, but they're working with a social matrix.

Interviewed by James J. Martine in
Critical Essays on Arthur Miller

Tragedy

I believe that the common man is as apt a subject for tragedy in its highest sense as kings were. On the face of it this ought to be obvious in the light of modern psychiatry, which bases its analysis upon classic formulations, such as the Oedipus and Orestes complexes, for instances, which were enacted by royal beings, but which apply to everyone in similar emotional situations.

More simply, when the question of tragedy in art is not at issue, we never hesitate to attribute to the well-placed and the exalted the very same mental processes as the lowly. And finally, if the exaltation of tragic action were truly a property of the high-bred character alone, it is inconceivable that the mass of mankind should cherish tragedy above all other forms, let alone be capable of understanding it.

As a general rule, to which there may be exceptions unknown to me, I think the tragic feeling is evoked in us when we are in the presence of a character who is ready to lay down his life, if need be, to secure one thing — his sense of personal dignity. From Orestes to Hamlet, Medea to Macbeth, the underlying struggle is that of the individual attempting to gain his 'rightful' position in his society. Sometimes he is one who has been displaced from it, sometimes one who seeks to attain it for the first time, but the fateful wound from which the inevitable events spiral is the wound of indignity, and its dominant force is indignation. Tragedy, then, is the consequence of a man's total compulsion to evaluate himself justly.

New York Times, 27 Feb. 1949

Radio Drama

The economy of words in a good radio play was everything. It drove you more and more to realize what the power of a good sentence was, and the right phrase could save you a page you would otherwise be wasting. I was always sorry radio didn't last long enough for contemporary poetic movements to take advantage of it, because it's a natural medium for poets. It's pure voice, pure words. Words and silence; a marvellous medium.

The Paris Review, X (Summer 1966), p. 61-98

On Jewishness

Jews can't afford to revel too much in the tragic because it might overwhelm them. Consequently, in most Jewish writing there's always the caution, 'Don't push it too far toward the abyss, because you're liable to fall in.' I think it's part of that psychology and it's part of me, too. I have, so to speak, a psychic investment in the continuity of life. I couldn't ever write a totally nihilistic work.

The Paris Review, X (Summer 1966), p. 61-98

By whatever means, I had somehow arrived at the psychological role of mediator between the Jews and America, and among Americans themselves as well. No doubt as a defence against the immensity of the domestic and European fascistic threat, which in my depths I interpreted as the threat of my own extinction, I had the wish, if not yet the conviction, that art could express the universality of human beings, their common emotions and ideas.

Timebends

American and European Drama

The net of it all was that serious writers could reasonably assume that they were addressing the whole American mix, and so their plays, whether successfully or not, stretched toward a wholeness of experience that would not require specialists or a coterie to be understood. As alienated a spirit as he was, O'Neill tried for the big audience, and Clifford Odets no less so, along with every other writer longing to prophesy to America, from Whitman and Melville to Dreiser and Hemingway and on.

For Europe's playwrights the situation was profoundly different, with society already split beyond healing between the working class and its allies, who were committed to a socialist destiny, and the bourgeois mentality that sought an art of reassurance and the pleasures of forgetting what was happening in the streets. (The first American plays I saw left me wondering where the characters came from. The people I knew were fanatics about surviving, but onstage everyone seemed to have mysteriously guaranteed incomes, and though every play had to have something about 'love', there was nothing about sex, which was all there was in Brooklyn, at least that I ever noticed.) An American avant-garde, therefore, if only because the domination of society by the middle class was profoundly unchallenged, could not simply steal from Brecht or even Shaw and expect its voice to reach beyond the small alienated minority that had arrived in their seats already converted to its aims. That was not the way to change the world.

For a play to do that it had to reach precisely those who accepted everything as it was; great drama is great questions or it is nothing but technique. I could not imagine a theatre worth my time that did not want to change the world, any more than a creative scientist could wish to prove the validity of everything that is already known. I knew only one other writer with the same approach, even if he surrounded his work with a far different aura. This was Tennessee Williams.

Timebends

The Theatre of the Absurd

In the early fifties the so-called theatre of the absurd was still in the offing, and I would resist most of its efforts as spurious, but each generation of writers has an investment in its accomplishments that it is obliged to defend.

Timebends

a: Primary Sources

Collection of Plays

Collected Plays, Volume One. New York: Viking, 1957;
    London: Cresset, 1958 (re-issued, Secker and Warburg,
    1974). [*All My Sons, Death of a Salesman, The Crucible,
    A Memory of Two Mondays, A View from the Bridge* (two-
    act version).]
Collected Plays, Volume Two. New York: Viking, 1981;
    London: Secker and Warburg, 1981. [*The Misfits, After the
    Fall, Incident at Vichy, The Price, The Creation of the
    World and Other Business, Playing for Time*.]
The Portable Arthur Miller. New York: Viking, 1971.
    [*Death of a Salesman, The Crucible, Incident at Vichy, The
    Price, The Misfits*.]

Articles and Essays

Collection

The Theatre Essays of Arthur Miller, ed. Robert A. Martin.
    New York: Viking, 1978. Harmondsworth: Penguin, 1978.

Individual Essays

'The Plaster Masks', *Encore*, IX (April 1946), p. 424-32.
'Subsidized Theatre', *The New York Times*, 22 June 1947,
    Sec. 2, p. 1.
'Tragedy and the Common Man', *The New York Times*,
    27 Feb. 1949, Sec. 2, p. 1, 3.
'Arthur Miller on 'The Nature of Tragedy', *New York Herald
    Tribune*, 27 Mar. 1949, Sec. 5, p. 1, 2.
'The *Salesman* Has a Birthday', *The New York Times*,
    5 Feb. 1950, Sec. 2, p. 1, 3.
'An American Reaction', *World Theatre*, I (1951), p. 21-2.
'Preface' to adaptation of Henrik Ibsen's *An Enemy of the
    People* (New York: Viking, 1951).
'Many Writers: Few Plays', *The New York Times*,
    10 Aug. 1952, Sec. 2, p. 1.
'Journey to *The Crucible*', *The New York Times*, 8 Feb. 1953,
    Sec. 2, p. 3.

'Universtiy of Michigan', *Holiday*, XIV (Dec. 1953),
p. 68-71, 128-34, 136-7, 140-3.

'A Modest Proposal for Pacification of the Public Temper', *The Nation*,
CLXXIX (3 July 1954), p. 5-8

'The American Theatre', *Holiday*, XVII (Jan. 1955), p. 90-8, 101-2,
104.

'A Boy Grew in Brooklyn', *Holiday*, XVII (Mar. 1955), p. 54-5, 117,
119-20, 122-4.

'Picking a Cast', *New York Times*, 21 Aug. 1955, Sec. 2, p. 1.

'On Social Plays', preface to *A View from the Bridge* (New York:
Viking, 1955).

'The Family in Modern Drama', *Atlantic Monthly*, CXCVII
(April 1956), p. 35-41.

'Concerning the Boom', *International Theatre Annual*, No. 1,
ed. Harold Hobson (London: John Calder, 1956), p. 85-8.

'The Playwright and the Atomic World', *Colorado Quarterly*, V
(Autumn 1956), p. 117-37; reprinted in *Tulane Drama Review*, V
(June 1961), p. 3-20.

'The Writer in America', *Mainstream*, X (July 1957), p. 43-6.

'Global Dramatist', *New York Times*, 21 July 1957, Sec. 2, p. 1.

'Introduction' to *Arthur Miller's Collected Plays* (New York: Viking,
1957).

'The Writer's Position in America', *Coastlines*, VII (Autumn 1957),
p. 38-40.

'Morality and Modern Drama', *Educational Theatre Journal*, X
(Oct. 1958), p. 190-202.

'Brewed in *The Crucible*', *New York Times*, 9 March 1958, Sec. 2, p. 3.

'The Shadows of the Gods', *Harper's*, CCXX (Nov. 1960), p. 63-9.

'Art and Commitment', *Anvil and Student Partisan*, XI (Winter 1960),
p. 5.

'Introduction' to *A View from the Bridge*, two-act version
(New York: Compass, 1960).

'The Playwright and the Atomic World' *Tulane Drama Review*, V
(June 1961), p. 3-20.

'The Bored and the Violent', *Harper's*, CCXXV (Nov. 1962), p. 50-2,
55-6.

'A New Era in American Theatre?' *Drama Survey*, III (Spring 1963),
p. 70-1.

'On Recognition', *Michigan Quarterly Review*, II (Autumn 1963),
p. 213-20.

'Lincoln Repertory Theater — Challenge and Hope', *New York Times*,
19 Jan. 1964, Sec. 2, p. 1, 3.

'Foreword' to *After the Fall*, *Saturday Evening Post*, CCXXXVII
(1 Feb. 1964), p. 32.

'With Respect for Her Agony — But with Love', *Life*, LVI
(7 Feb. 1964), p. 66. [On *After the Fall*.]

'Death of a Salesman', in *Playwrights on Playwriting*, ed. Toby Cole.
(New York: Hill and Wang, 1964), p. 261-76.

'Our Guilt for the World's Evil', *New York Times Magazine*,
3 Jan. 1965, p. 10-11, 48.

'*After the Fall*: an Author's View', *New Haven Register*, 25 Apr. 1965,
p. 9.

'What Makes Plays Endure?', *New York Times*, 15 Aug. 1965, Sec. 2,
p. 1, 3.

'Our Guilt for the World Evil', *New York Times*, 3 Jan. 1965, p. 10-11,
48.

'Arthur Miller: PEN, Politics and Literature', *Publisher's Weekly*, CXC
(18 July 1966), p. 32-3.

'Literature and Mass Communication', *World Theatre*, XV (1966),
p. 164-7.

'It Could Happen Here — and Did', *New York Times*, 30 Apr. 1967,
Sec. 2, p. 17.

'The Contemporary Theater', *Michigan Quarterly Review*, VI
(Summer 1967), p. 153-63.

'The Age of Abdication', *New York Times*, 23 Dec. 1967, p. 22.

'The New Insurgency', *The Nation*, CCVI (3 June 1968), p. 717.

'Writers in Prison', *Encounter*, XXX (June 1968), p. 60-1.

'On the Shooting of Robert Kennedy', *The New York Times*,
8 June 1968, p. 30.

'The Battle of Chicago: from the Delegates' Side', *New York Times
Magazine*, 15 Sept. 1968, p. 29-31, 122, 124, 126, 128.

'Are We Interested in Stopping the Killing?' *New York Times*,
8 June 1969, Sec. 2, p. 21.

'Broadway from O'Neill to Now', *New York Times*, 21 Dec. 1969,
Sec. 2, p. 3, 7.

'The Bangkok Prince', *Harper's*, CCXLI (July 1970), p. 32-3.

'The War between Young and Old, or Why Willy Loman Can't
Understand What's Happening', *McCall's*, XCVII (July 1970), p. 32.

'Banned in Russia', *New York Times*, 10 Dec. 1970, p. 47.

'When Life Had at Least a Form', *New York Times*, 24 Jan. 1971, p. 17.

'Men and Words in Prison', *New York Times*, 16 Oct. 1971, p. 29.

'Arthur Miller on *The Crucible*', *Audience*, II (July-Aug. 1972), p. 46-7.

'Making Crowds', *Esquire*, LXXVII (Nov. 1972), p. 160-1, 216, 218,
220, 222, 224, 226, 228.

'Politics as Theater', *New York Times*, 4 Nov. 1972, p. 33.

'Miracles', *Esquire*, LXXX (Sept. 1973), p. 112-15, 202-4.

'On True Identity', *New York Times Magazine*, 13 Apr. 1975, p. 111.

'The Prague Writer', *New York Times*, 16 July 1975, p. 37.

'Toward a New Foreign Policy', *Society*, XIII (March-April 1976),
  p. 10, 15, 16.
'The American Writer: the American Theater', in *The Writer's Craft:
  Hopwood lectures 1965-81*, ed. Robert A. Martin (Ann Arbor:
  Michigan University Press, 1982), p. 254-70.

Selected Interviews

John K. Hutchens, 'Mr. Miller Has a Change of Luck',
  New York Times, 23 Feb. 1947, Sec. 2, p. 1, 3.
Ira Wolfert, 'Arthur Miller, Playwright in Search of His Identity',
  New York Herald Tribune, 25 Jan. 1953, Sec. 4, p. 3.
John and Alice Griffen, 'Arthur Miller, Discusses *The Crucible*',
  Theatre Arts, XXXVII (Oct. 1953), p. 33-4.
Dorothy and Joseph Samachson, in *Let's Meet the Theatre*
  (New York: Abelard-Schuman, 1954), p. 15-20.
'*Death of a Salesman*: a Symposium', *Tulane Drama Review*, II
  (May 1958), p. 63-9.
Phillip Gelb, 'Morality and Modern Drama', *Educational Theatre
  Journal*, X (Oct. 1958), p. 190-202.
Kenneth Allsop, 'A Conversation with Arthur Miller', *Encounter*,
  XIII (July 1959), p. 58-60.
Henry Brandon, 'The State of the Theatre', *Harper's*, CCXXI
  (Nov. 1960), p. 63-9.
Walter Wager, 'Arthur Miller', in *The Playwrights Speak*,
  ed. Walter Wager (New York: Dell, 1967), p. 1-24.
Barbara Gelb, 'Question: Am I My Brother's Keeper?' *New York Times*,
  29 Nov. 1964, Sec. 2, p. 1, 3.
Sheridan Morley, 'Miller on Miller', *Theatre World*, LXI (March 1965),
  p. 4-8.
Olga Carlisle and Rose Styron, 'Arthur Miller: an Interview',
  Paris Review, X (Summer 1966), p. 61-98; reprinted in
  Writers at Work: the Paris Review Interviews, Third Series,
  ed. George Plimpton (New York: Viking, 1968), p. 197-230.
'Arthur Miller Talks Again: a Chat with a Class in Stage Directing',
  Michigan Quarterly Review, VI (Summer 1967), p. 178-84.
Joan Barthel, 'Arthur Miller Ponders *The Price*', *New York Times*,
  28 Jan. 1968, Sec. 2, p. 1, 5.
Robert A. Martin, 'The Creative Experience of Arthur Miller: an
  Interview', *Educational Theatre Journal*, XXI (Oct. 1969),
  p. 310-17.
Robert A. Martin, 'Arthur Miller and the Meaning of Tragedy',
  Modern Drama, XIII (Summer 1970), p. 34-9.

Rust Hills, 'Conversation: Arthur Miller and William Styron', *Audience*, I (Nov.-Dec. 1971), p. 6-21.

Mel Gussow, 'Arthur Miller Returns to Genesis for First Musical', *New York Times*, 17 Apr. 1974, p. 37.

Robert W. Corrigan, 'Interview: Arthur Miller', *Michigan Quarterly Review*, XIII (Fall 1974), p. 401-5.

Robert A. Martin and Richard D. Meyer, 'Arthur Miller on Plays and Playwriting', *Modern Drama*, XIX (Dec. 1976), p. 375-84.

Christian-Albrecht Gollub, 'Interview with Arthur Miller', *Michigan Quarterly Review*, XVI (Spring 1977), p. 121-41.

Arthur Miller, 'Every Play has a Purpose', *Dramatists Guild Quarterly*, XV (Winter 1979), p. 13-20.

James J. Martine, 'All in a Boiling Soup', in *Critical Essays on Arthur Miller*, ed. James J. Martine (Boston: G. K. Hall, 1979).

Arthur Miller, 'Learning from a Performer: a Conversation with Arthur Miller', *Gamut*, I (1982), p. 9-23.

'The Will to Live: an Interview with Arthur Miller', *Modern Drama*, XXVII (1984), p. 345-60.

Christopher Bigsby, 'Miller's Odyssey to a Brutal Decade', *The Guardian*, 4 Aug. 1986, p. 9.

Michael Ratcliffe, 'Miller's Russian Tale', *The Observer*, 26 Oct. 1986, p. 23.

b: Secondary Sources

Collections of Essays

Gerald Weales, ed., *Arthur Miller: 'Death of a Salesman': Text and Criticism*. New York: Viking, 1967.

Robert W. Corrigan, ed., *Arthur Miller: a Collection of Critical Essays*. Englewood Cliffs, N.J.: Prentice-Hall, 1969.

Gerald Weales, ed., *Arthur Miller: 'The Crucible': Text and Criticism*. New York: Viking, 1971.

John H. Ferres, ed., *Twentieth Century Interpretations of 'The Crucible'*. Englewood Cliffs, N.J.: Prentice-Hall, 1972.

Walter J. Meserve, ed., *The Merrill Studies in 'Death of a Salesman'*. Columbus, Ohio: Merrill, 1972.

James J. Martine, ed., *Critical Essays on Arthur Miller*. Boston: Hall, 1979.

Helen W. Koon, ed., *'Death of a Salesman': a Collection of Critical Essays*. Englewood-Cliffs, N.J.: Prentice-Hall, 1983.

Full-Length Studies

Dennis Welland, *Arthur Miller*. Edinburgh; London: Oliver and Boyd; New York: Grove, 1961.

Robert Hogan, *Arthur Miller*. Minneapolis: University of Minnesota Press, 1964.

Sheila Huftel, *Arthur Miller: the Burning Glass*. New York: Citadel, 1965.

Leonard Moss, *Arthur Miller*. New York: Twayne, 1967.

Edward Murray, *Arthur Miller, Dramatist*. New York: Ungar, 1967.

Robert W. Corrigan, ed., *Arthur Miller: a Collection of Critical Essays*. Englewood Cliffs, N.J.: Prentice-Hall, 1969.

Richard I. Evans and Arthur Miller, *Psychology and Arthur Miller*. New York: Dutton, 1969.

Benjamin Nelson, *Arthur Miller: Portrait of a Playwright*. London: Peter Owen, 1970.

Ronald Hayman, *Arthur Miller*. New York: Ungar, 1972.

Dennis Welland, *Miller: a Study of His Plays*. London: Eyre Methuen, 1979; rev. ed. 1983.

Robert A. Martin, ed., *Arthur Miller: New Perspectives*. Englewood Cliffs, N.J.: Prentice-Hall, 1982.

Neil Carson, *Arthur Miller*. London: Macmillan, 1982.

Articles and Chapters in Books

Eric Bentley, 'Back to Broadway', *Theatre Arts*, XXXII (Nov. 1949), p. 10-15.

Daniel E. Schneider, *The Psychoanalyst and the Artist*. New York: Farrar, Straus, 1950.

David W. Sievers, *Freud on Broadway: a History of Psychoanalysis and the American Drama*. New York: Farrar, Straus, 1950.

John Gassner, *The Theatre in Our Times*. New York: Crown, 1954.

David W. Sievers, Freud on Broadway: a History of Psychoanalysis and the American Drama. New York: Hermitage, 1955.

John Gassner, *Form and Idea in Modern Theatre*. New York: Dryden, 1956.

Harold Clurman, *Lies Like Truth*. New York: Grove, 1958.

Raymond Williams, 'The Realism of Arthur Miller', *Critical Quarterly*, I (1959), p. 34-7.

Elia Kazan, *A Theater in Your Head*. New York: Funk and Wagnalls, 1960. [Excerpts from his notebooks for *Death of a Salesman*.]

Tom Driver, 'Strength and Weakness in Arthur Miller', *Tulane Drama Review*, IV (May 1960), p. 45-52.

M. W. Steinberg, 'Arthur Miller and the Idea of Modern Tragedy',

Dalhousie Review, XL (1961), p. 329-40.

John D. Hurrell, ed., *Two Modern Tragedies: Reviews and Criticism of 'Death of a Salesman' and 'A Streetcar Named Desire'*. New York: Scribners, 1961.

John Prudoe, 'Arthur Miller and the Tradition of Tragedy', *English Studies*, XLIII (1962), p. 430-9.

Esther M. Jackson, '*Death of a Salesman*: Tragic Myth in the Modern Theatre', *College Language Association Journal*, VII (Sept. 1963), p. 63-76.

Robert Brustein, 'Arthur Miller's Mea Culpa', *New Republic*, CL (Feb. 1964), p. 26-30.

Harold Clurman, 'Director's Notes: *Incident at Vichy*', *Tulane Drama Review*, IX (Summer 1965), p. 79-90.

Richard D. and Nancy Meyer, '*After the Fall*: a View from the Director's Notebook', *Theatre*, II (1965), p. 43-73.

Javier Coy, 'Arthur Miller: Notas para una interpretacion sociologica', *Filologia Moderna*, XXIII-XXIV (1966), p. 299-312.

Peter Buitenhuis, 'Arthur Miller: the Fall from the Bridge', *Canadian Association for American Studies Bulletin*, III (1967), p. 55-71.

C. W. E. Bigsby, *Confrontation and Commitment: a Study of Contemporary American Drama 1959-66*. London: McGibbon and Kee; Columbia: University of Missouri Press, 1967.

Ruby Cohn, *Dialogue in American Drama*. Bloomington: Indiana University Press, 1971.

Ralph W. Willett, 'A Note on Arthur Miller's *The Price*', *Journal of American Studies*, V (1971), p. 307-10.

Morris Freedman, *American Drama in Social Context*. Carbondale: Southern Illinois University Press, 1971.

Robert W. Corrigan, *The Theatre in Search of a Fix*. New York: Delacorte, 1973.

Dan Vogel, *The Three Masks of American Tragedy*. Baton Rouge: Louisiana State University Press, 1974.

Hans Itschert, in *Das amerikanische Drama*, ed. Paul Goetsch (Düsseldorf: Bagel, 1974).

Larry W. Cook, 'The Function of Ben and Dave Singleman in *Death of a Salesman*', *Notes on Contemporary Literature*, V (January 1975), p. 7-9.

Orm Overland, 'The Action and its Significance: Arthur Miller's Struggle with Dramatic Form', *Modern Drama*, XVII (1975), p. 1-14.

Miklos Vajda, 'Arthur Miller: Moralist as Playwright', *New Hungarian Quarterly*, XVI (1975), p. 171-80.

Lawrence D. Lowenthal, 'Arthur Miller's *Incident at Vichy*: a Sartrean Interpretation', *Modern Drama*, XVIII (1975), p. 29-41.

Tony Manocchio and William Petitt, 'The Loman Family', in *Families Under Stress: A Psychological Interpretation*. London: Routledge, 1975.

Herbert Grabes, ed., *Das amerikanische Drama der Gegenwart*. Athenäum, 1976.

Robert A. Martin, 'Arthur Miller's *The Crucible*: Background and Sources', *Modern Drama*, XX (1977), p. 279-92.

Tom Scanlan, *Family, Drama, and American Dreams*. Westport, Conn.: Greenwood, 1978.

Karl Harshbarger, *The Burning Jungle: an Analysis of Arthur Miller's 'Death of a Salesman'*. Washington, DC: University Press of America, 1978.

Einar Haugen, 'Ibsen as Fellow Traveler: Arthur Miller's Adaptation of *An Enemy of the People*', *Scandinavian Studies*, LI (1979), p. 343-53.

Robert N. Wilson, *The Writer as Social Seer*. Chapel Hill: University of North Carolina Press, 1979.

William J. McGill Jr., 'The Crucible of History: Arthur Miller's John Proctor', *New England Quarterly*, LIV, No. 2 (June 1981), p. 258-64.

Enoch Prater, 'Ethics and Ethnicity in the Plays of Arthur Miller', in *From Hester Street to Hollywood: the Jewish-American Stage and Screen*, ed. Sarah Blacher Cohen (Bloomington: Indiana University Press, 1983).

C. W. E. Bigsby, *A Critical Introduction to Twentieth Century American Drama*, Vol. 2. Cambridge: Cambridge University Press, 1984.

E. Miller Budick, 'History and Other Spectres in Arthur Miller's *The Crucible*', *Modern Drama*, XXVII (1985), p. 535-52.

Reference Sources

Leonard Moss, *Arthur Miller*. New York: Twayne, 1967.

Benjamin Nelson, *Arthur Miller: Portrait of a Playwright*. London: Peter Owen, 1970.

Robert A Martin, ed., *The Theater Essays of Arthur Miller*. New York, 1978.

Charles A. Carpenter, 'Studies of Arthur Miller's Drama: a Selective International Bibliography, 1966-1979', in *Arthur Miller: New Perspectives*, ed. Robert A. Martin (Englewood Cliffs, N.J.: Prentice-Hall, 1982).

Dennis Welland, *Miller: the Playwright*, third ed. London: Methuen, 1985.